PRAISE OF MARK A. HOLLINGSWORTH'S WRITING CULLED
FROM THOUSANDS OF COMMENTS ON HIS BLOG...

The story is not only heart-breaking and sobering... but it is one of the most superb, vivid pieces of writing I have ever read, written with so much honesty and passion. It's like I was there, seeing what you saw... feeling what you felt. It took my breath away. That piece needs to be read by everyone... at least by every American. You should write a book. And you should definitely be on Oprah. I'm going to forward that article to her producers.   -A.B.

If the mark of good writing is that people identify with it, then this is a masterpiece. A thousand "Amens!"   -R.P.

I was so moved by your story. I just wanted to say thank you for sharing it. I made the mistake of reading it at work. First, I couldn't stop crying, and then I couldn't (and still can't) stop thinking about it. But I don't want to stop thinking about it. You told the story so eloquently and so painfully.   -K.E.

That has to be the funniest flying story ever told! Thanks for letting me laugh at your pain. Too bad you didn't write it twenty years ago; it should've been included in *Planes, Trains, and Automobiles*.   -R.T.

Once again, Mark—your writing feeds my creative and spiritual DNA!   -R.I.

I'm speechless but filled with something so great I feel I could burst. Tears have trickled down my face for the past fifteen minutes. I'm appalled, disgusted, helpless, sad, grateful, happy, and proud... What a beautiful, beautiful, beautiful story. I'm still at a loss for words and appropriate elaborations. Your soul is a precious, powerful force in this world. God bless you.   -A.

You have a poignancy in your writing that captures such unique experiences and often expresses a viewpoint from a place I haven't walked... and that makes it all the more valuable to me. It helps put perspective on life.   -R.C.

Thanks for sharing so personally. Your willingness to talk of weakness is a great strength.   -G.L.

What a great story! Ha! And yet, a little disturbing! Yes, very brave of you to admit some of the details, but that's one of the things I like... your honesty. I kept imagining this as a movie scene played out by Ben Stiller. What a hoot! -G.T.

I continue to be moved and amazed by all you've experienced... George Plimpton ain't got nothin' on you, my friend.   -M.N.

Oh my ever-loving God. I'm speechless. Thanks for the soul chiropractic adjustment. Wow. This is deep, candid, honest stuff.   -G.B.

I so appreciate the openness in your writing. It's refreshing to read your words. Many followers of Christ have had the same struggles and ask the same questions... I know I have and sometimes still do. The "church" is often put off by deep questions and the back-and-forth debate that can cross our minds and hearts. AND... You really should write a book! It's a thought provoking work and shines a light into an area that remains pretty dark.   -K.

You are a master storyteller, and you've lived a story well worth telling. I greatly admire your willingness to reveal such thoughts, showing us your humanity. You put into words what many of us have experienced in some shape or form, in a truly profound way.   -W.H.

Have appreciated this story so much and have eagerly awaited each installment! I felt like a Londoner in the nineteenth century waiting for the latest chapter of the new Charles Dickens novel. You are a great writer and I am looking forward to your book.   -G.S.

I'm not a religious person, but altruism doesn't have a label. This story was very touching.   -F.M.

There are no words that remain; you have aptly used them each at their proper time and in their most beautiful form. Thank you for sharing your heart and for the profound reminder.   -L.M.

I wish I could give at least twenty kudos. My stomach hurts from laughing so hard, and my mascara is running down my cheeks!   -A.D.

After all this and more, God has put it on your heart to share this intense and dramatic proof that "truth is stranger than fiction" with others—that they (we) may gain insight and inspiration from your courage and fortitude—and it becomes clear that when your hand is called, you have no reason not to put "all your cards on the table."   -P.G.

Incredible story, Mark. Very stirring. I love it when something makes me think. So often, we go through life with blinders on. Thanks for the kick in the arse. Time to get creative.   -J.

Ahhh. I LOVE this, Mark. So, when are you going to compile all your thoughtful, heart-full musings into a book so I can page through and enjoy them at leisure anytime?   -D.S.

True, fascinating, humorous and heartfelt… like a John Hughes movie. He would have liked it… I sure did.   -L.L.

I am moved, not by the persuasiveness of the argument, though effective and sound, but rather by the beautiful picture of a caring, faithful friend, shepherding a brother through turbulent waters.   -S.F.

Wonderful piece of writing on so many levels. You have related the macro and micro-cosmic scales of the traveler's life—and the pilgrim's—remarkably well here. So much contrast, so many parallels, and so much like my own point of view. I'll have to re-read this to get a full appreciation of all the images and subtle shades you paint. Well worth the time; well worth it.   -K.L.E.

Mark, thanks for your grace-filled ability to both challenge and encourage us at the same time.   -V.W.

It's interesting to see how your life has twisted and turned even while you've walked on the "straight & narrow" path. And those you've met along the way have made it just that much more interesting of a trip.   -B.H.

This is exactly what I need to read right now. You know of my struggles, and to know you had them too means the world to me. I look forward to more of your words.   -A.

Wow. Your stories are a great reminder of what is really important in life and that it can all be gone in literally a split-second. Powerful stuff.   -E.

Once again sir, you have the uncanny ability to make light of what was a trau-matic situation. I enjoy reading your writing, because you are able to take some of the worst situations and use humor in a way that I *feel* that I should feel sorry for you, but I can't stop laughing.   -B.N.

I have tears running down my face as I read this. How miraculous... how spec-tacular... how humbling.   -A.B.

Write a book already!   -J.W.

Bill—
From one musical sojourner to
another.... keep asking the deep
questions. *Cheers—*

16.7.10

EMBRACING THE GRAY

Mark Hollingsworth

A Wing, A Prayer, and
A Doubter's Resolve

MARK A. HOLLINGSWORTH

Cover design by Suzanna Spring Graphic Design.
Front cover photo: "A Wing and a Prayer," ©2007, Mark A. Hollingsworth
Back cover photo: "Jetsam That Has Been Flotsammed," ©1988, Mark A. Hollingsworth
To keep identities anonymous, some names have been changed.

International Standard Book Number: 978-1-60494-417-4
Library of Congress Control Number: 2010920693

For more on Mark A. Hollingsworth's bio, writing, travel, blog, correspondence, etc. please visit:
www.MarkAHollingsworth.com
www.Facebook.com/HollingsworthMark
www.MySpace.com/MarkHollingsworth

CONTENTS

Preface. xi

PART ONE: OBSOLETE ABSOLUTES

1. The Barrier 3
2. There Are No Accidents 'Round Here 6
3. Black Sheep 12
4. Flocks in Flux 20
5. Declaration of Separation 25
6. Darkness Around and Within 32
7. Enacting the Masque 37
8. Encountering the Wall 44
9. A Strange Aberration 50
10. Not Human Enough 58
11. Stripped But Not Afraid. 65
12. Taming a Mountain Ram 71
13. Shorn 77
14. In a Highlands Meadow. 83

PART TWO: SHADOWS AND LIGHT

15. Stuckey's Warm Fuzzies 93
16. I Shoulda Kissed Her 97
17. If You Really Wanna Die, Let Me Help You 105
18. The First Time I Met U2. 116
19. A Bellowing Babe and Handy Dandies over Cartagena . . .123
20. The Eternal Now 130
21. Checkers 140
22. Cold Cuts and Knifing Winds 148
23. Sleeping with Marc Wozniak 155

PART THREE: WHAT IS AND WHAT SHOULD BE

24. The Why in Wyoming .163
25. Ti Chape 168
26. Oh, Ya Got Trouble 176
27. Pounding Rocks. 182
28. Mercy in Mathere Valley 186
29. Entertaining Angels 192
30. Through Your Hands .199
31. Gray Matters. 212

Acknowledgements. 219
Notes/Bibliography 227

To Dave "Captain Tangent" Bunker:
Deep appreciation for all the marathon heart-to-hearts
through these many years,
and for inspiring me with the title
from your poem of the same name.

PREFACE

Thursday, Feb. 15th, 1996... another mid-south battleship gray morning. As is my daily tradition, I'm perusing the *Nashville Tennessean* in my bathrobe at my combo dining room table/office desk while scooping away on a bowl of raisin bran.

I've read newspapers since I was a kid, enjoying some semblance of keeping abreast of the local and global news, comparing the vitriol of various editorials, pondering reviews of art, film, and literature, and even updating the latest sports stats rolling around in my head. The internet offers all the same and even more. But the tactile feel of newsprint on thin, crackling paper has always been my preference.

Section D is the "Living" segment, with the bold heading of "Test Your GQ (Gusto Quotient)" front and center. Tim Harrower of Gannett News poses the subtitle: "When they film the movie version of your life, will it be a thriller or a snooze?" In the next few paragraphs, he teases by questioning whether my life has been interesting...even intriguing. Have I grabbed for gusto, or have I settled into some boring, repetitive mode?

He then unfolds a series of ninety questions with accompanying points and demerits in categories like Trotting the Globe, The Sporting Life, Into the Unknown, Everyday Drama, Fame and Fortune, Death and Disaster, and The Other Side.

I ponder the categories and consider my current situation: It's been several months since I was laid-off from my primary job at a record label, but I'm making ends meet by consulting with rock bands and pro sports leagues and franchises, as well as writing a monthly column on hockey marketing. I'm covering expenses, but there's a sense of ill-ease about how I've arrived at this point. I've also recently broken up from what seemed to be a marriage-bound relationship, and I wonder if I will ever find love again. I'm pretty much drifting with no clear sense of where I might be headed next. Some might even think I'm mildly depressed. I know there are some days when I feel like my life hasn't amounted to much and that I'm certainly not adding anything substantial to anyone else's, either.

I generally loathe these sorts of personal acumen quizzes in *People*, or *US*, or what-have-you. When you are already in a lumpy gravy mood, these usually only serve to make one feel even more blasé. But figuring it might help jolt me out of my doldrums, I grab a pen and start circling answers to multiple choice questions as varied as:

Have you ever piloted an airplane, helicopter, or hot air balloon? (Yes) 10 points.

Have you ever hiked or biked more than 100 miles in one trip? (Yes) 10 points.

Have you ever seen a UFO? (Yes) 10 points (add 50 if abducted). Ummm...no.

Have you ever taken part in a public protest? (Yes) 5 points.

Have you ever visited a nude beach, nudist colony, or appeared nude in public? (Yes) 5 points.

Have you ever been the subject of a magazine or newspaper story? (Yes) 10 points

Have you ever visited a foreign country? (Yes—a lot) 2 points per country.

Have you ever been arrested or detained? (Yes) 10 points.

Have you ever been involved in a high speed chase? (Yes) 5 points.

You get the idea. At the bottom of the page he has a system for gauging your Gusto Quotient:

0-100 points: You've lived a quieter, gentler life than some, but don't feel bad. We all can't be Indiana Jones.

101-200 points: An impressive start. Now it's time to turn off the TV, get up off the couch, and start racking ups some serious points.

201-300: Quite awesome. You are probably known as a "colorful character" who is lots of fun at parties, full of rousing tales and anecdotes. Either that or you cheated.

Over 300: Wow! Consider yourself lucky to be alive. At this rate, you'd better finish that autobiography fast.

I figured I would end up in the 250 range. I was amused to see that my total was actually 354. Perhaps my life wasn't such a drag after all. I've written many music reviews, press releases, editorials, and feature articles that have been printed in a couple dozen publications over the years ranging from *Radio and Records* to *National Lampoon*. Heck, I was even editor for an underground satire/comedy rag that was banned in my high school. Several folks have encouraged me to write about my experiences, both sordid and sacred, and I did some scribbling from time to time that I would dump into a file cabinet along with that *Tennessean* questionnaire.

Fast forward nine years to 2005. I'm back working for an international development outreach that has added more travel and bountiful experiences. I've loved and lost some more. I've grieved more deaths. I've celebrated more life-affirming relationships.

Some friends encouraged me to start MySpace and then Facebook pages with adjoining blogs. I printed a few of my pieces I had built up over those nine years, and I began weekly entries on subjects some might consider profane—others that some might think preachy, but mostly I just recounted sketches of my own narrative, trying to be as confessional as possible. More than anything, the discipline of writing and cataloguing my life has been therapeutic; it's become a way of planting landmarks. By recounting what happened and giving definition to it, I've been able to better learn. I guess it struck a chord with some along the way, as the blog has had over 50,000 readers in less than five years. Among the several thousand comments, some have even suggested I compile my thoughts into book form.

Not long ago, I pulled out that questionnaire and retook it. The total has now climbed to 462.

So, here goes...

PART ONE

OBSOLETE ABSOLUTES

CHAPTER 1

THE BARRIER

It was the summer of my sophomore year of high school the first time I had the dream. I rarely remember my nocturnal visions, and even the ones I do recall upon awakening most often dissipate like stroked Windex on warm glass—seen, yet soon evaporated. But this apparition stayed with me and revisited every few months.

I'm traveling fairly low to the ground… perhaps on foot but more as if slightly levitating. My point of view is that of being on the front bumper of a vehicle churning over predominantly flat terrain; in the twilight netherworld that could either be pre-dawn or dusk. A dusty mist fills the air. The horizon between the earth and sky is delineated by something, and I am moving toward it…or am I being drawn?

If I look to my left, it seems to disappear in the distance. The same when I glance to the right. Behind me is growing darkness, and I don't feel any inclination to go back. I'm constantly leaning forward, out of curiosity as much as anything.

Some moments in the specter, I am hurtling ahead at super-sonic speeds. However; just as suddenly, there are times where I seem not only to drop out of hyperspace but churn as if stuck—or

worse, sinking. Most of the time, though, there's a sense of momen-
tum; there's marked headway.

Growing larger ahead of me is some sort of barrier. The swirling
elements often play with the depth perception. At first it seems not
to be that high and may only be a few hundred yards away. But as
the relative speed and distance suggests, it's actually much farther,
and hence, larger than what I can easily perceive.

Even though the phantasm has returned with some regularity
over the years, there are times in the dream that I don't seem to
make any progress whatsoever, or I will be dropped in some slightly
different path but still headed toward that wall in the gloaming.

As the vision continues, the obstacle comes into more focused
view. When making good speed on relatively unobstructed topography, I could begin studying what lie ahead, much like one might
observe cloud patterns while driving down a straight freeway.
I notice that to the left, the barricade seems to be lighter in hue.
To the right, it is much darker. Actually, it is white and black. And
where the two seem to intersect, there's a clear demarcation. In
fact, if I aim my heading in just the proper alignment, there's a slice
of intense light emanating from between (or is it behind?) the two
halves. Sometimes that razor thin shaft is visible from an angle as it
illuminates dust and debris blowing through its beam. But usually
it's only perceptible if I am centered squarely, letting it dissect right
between my eyes. If it hits either pupil directly, it's too intense, and
the resultant squinting causes me to lose focus, and eventually my
navigation suffers.

In some recurrences of the sleepy trance, I steer more toward
the white. And others I seem drawn towards the black. Either way,
I'm advancing forward. But my curiosity is most peaked when
aiming for that bright centrum…or is it being led in by that steady
but oft-elusive homing beacon? The black, the white, the path, the

light...are all elements of my story, and it's being defined because of—and often despite—them.

Over the decades, I've had the dream during peaceful vacations in Hawaii and the German Alps. I've had it while flying through the Bermuda Triangle or over the tundra of upper Manitoba. I've had this deep-night re-visitation while wrestling with extreme health issues, job transitions, and grief. It's usually unexpected but has come to be welcomed as a sort of assurance that, despite its mystery, I am being summoned to keep aiming, keep churning, and keep on keeping on.

CHAPTER 2

THERE ARE NO ACCIDENTS
'ROUND HERE

There is a time for everything
And a season for every activity under heaven
A time to be born and a time to die
(Ecclesiastes 3: 1-2)

Late yesterday, I was driving to downtown Nashville for dinner with some radio industry associates after spending a leisurely afternoon with my some friends. We had shared lunch, discussing music, jobs, and relationships. Then we watched *Ladder 49*, and were reminded of the sudden shifts that our lives can take...that even when giving sacrificially, Karma does not always work out the way we might expect. This was pulsing through my mind as I motored along.

Having rained much of the afternoon, the roadways were still shimmering from sharp shafts of sunlight perforating broken clouds. I was nearly trance-like from the simple beauty of it all: the bursting buds of spring-life on the ground... the azure sky parting the firmament. With windows down, everything smelled as fresh and clean as it appeared. It was one of those existential moments…. I sensed God wanting to get my attention somehow…that there was something I needed to know…to experience.

As I entered the Capitol District, on a whim I decided to turn down a street I rarely traverse. After all, this was a Sunday afternoon drive, wasn't it? I thought it would be interesting to see if any new structures were in place near the Bicentennial Mall, being a fan of the architectural revival in that part of town. As I approached James Robertson Parkway, the vista of the skyline was framed in the most stunning blue horizon. I even noticed how green the traffic light appeared in contrast to the sky.

Just as I was about to pass through that normally busy intersection, I was startled to see out of my peripheral vision to my left, a silver Honda hurtling down the road going at least 50 mph, completely oblivious to the red light. He was on course to broadside me—and hard. Slamming my brakes, my Mitsubishi slipped on the moist pavement. I came to a sliding stop after about twenty feet, and the other driver—suddenly awakened out of his stupor—swerved wildly. We avoided colliding by no more than six inches. His speed carried him well beyond our near meeting point; and being embarrassed, I guess, he decided to flee from further possible trouble.

I looked in my rear view mirror to see an SUV that had nearly rear-ended me in the fiasco. I raised my arms as if to say, "What the…?" He concurred with my gesture, as did the pilot of another car passing through the intersection from the opposite direction. I was rattled. It all happened in the snap of a finger. If I had been passing through that interchange just *one* second earlier, I would be in a morgue now.

Driving the final eight blocks to my destination, my wits were jangled from what could have easily been my quick demise. Just

1,000 feet from where I needed to park, I began to turn onto Commerce Street when a young touristy looking guy stepped right into my path. He was chatting with some friends and was simply not paying heed. Once again I jammed my brake pedal, screeching loudly. Had I been going just 3 mph faster, or had he taken just one more stride, I would've most certainly mashed both his kneecaps, and quite possibly would've crushed him. As before, it all occurred instantaneously.

Upon arriving at my parking lot, I sat and pondered. Just like it was yesterday, I recalled from twenty-two years ago, a similar experience...

Having just closed a major promotional deal that was going to bring me tens of thousands of dollars, I was returning to my home on a drizzly afternoon on the south inner-loop around Nashville. As I crested a rise in the freeway, I saw a car around 500 yards ahead of me acting erratically. It took a sudden left, did a couple of 360's and slammed hard into the center median. Eighteen-wheelers and service trucks were veering madly to avoid hitting the wayward vehicle. I started to slow down, being careful not to lock my brakes and go into a long slide on the slick asphalt.

Then the driver of the runaway wreck did the most frightening thing: she began to accelerate toward the onrushing traffic. This was a scene right out of *The Blues Brothers*, but it wasn't funny.... She was coming straight at me, and I had burgeoning big rigs on either side of me. They, in turn, had traffic on their sides as well. I was in the middle lane of a five wide expressway—with no options. She was headed toward me like Pharaoh's chariots trying to outrun the walls of the Red Sea crashing down upon them. Throwing any caution to the wind, I now applied full pressure to my disc brakes and unfortunately went into a headlong slide.

I can attest that in certain moments like these, your life does indeed pass before your eyes. Something triggered deep in my soul, and I sensed a lot about my life at that very instant. Money didn't mean a sturdy turd. Closing the big deal meant little. Success was a mere fleeting fancy. Being recognized as "an industry leader" was worthless compared with just wanting to stay alive.

My focus became so intense that everything seemed to begin moving in slow motion. I placed full weight on my brakes, hoping they would somehow grab hard onto some little speck of dry blacktop. Her car, which I now recognized as a metallic red Buick, finally appeared to be slowing in its crazed movements. With all this surging energy around me, I kept pounding my pedal. Some adhesion finally took hold, and two careening vessels that had been approaching each other at a combined 100 miles per hour just five seconds before were now nearing contact. I shall never forget those final ten feet...agonizing not so much about the impending collision, but fearing that in our subsequent spin into the other lanes, we would be obliterated by the waves of motorized metal streaming past us. But when impact occurred, it was literally the wispiest of love taps. Just the slightest little tick. And for what seemed like an eternity, I couldn't breath.

This young woman had a look of contorted horror on her face. She was in some sort of shock. With rush hour traffic slashing past us with all their horned accompaniment, we found ourselves in quite the pickle. Her car with two flat tires and facing the wrong direction...my car kissing hers. With the pungent smell of burning rubber still filling the air, I jumped out of my car to try and help her. Hysterical would not begin to explain her state. She wailed that she had freaked out and kept hitting the gas when she had really meant to be using her brakes. I tried calming her down, reasoning with her that we couldn't wait for the police to show up in this kind of traffic. We had to take matters into our own hands.

Without much thought, I decided I should try and stop all five lanes of traffic so she could try to turn around and limp over to the side of the road where a public service vehicle could then help her. Looking back on it now, I must have been out of my ever-loving mind. One super tanker refused to slow and just missed me by no more than twenty inches. Another van had no intention of varying its course in the least, and I dodged him via a watusi back step. With my heart pounding in my ears like a Ginger Baker drum solo, I somehow initially managed to wave traffic around us, then once getting the parade to slow down, actually convinced the subsequent rows to stop altogether.

Through tear-flushed eyes, she wobbled her big boat over to the south side of the freeway.

There was no time to exchange names or phone numbers for insurance purposes. I had to negotiate the moving obstacle course again to get back to my stalled car in the middle of the maelstrom. We were just two people that had nearly died together but would never connect again. I then ran back to my car and began easing forward. I must've looked like some sort of off-track pace car for the world's biggest race as vehicles of every shape and size were building up their own speed behind me.

About thirty seconds after I was back to normal highway speed, a strange sensation overtook me: I began to shake uncontrollably. The sheer intensity of what just happened had finally caught up with me, and I was going into some sort of shock of my own. Getting off at the next ramp, I pulled into a gas station, and I shook like a leaf for a couple of minutes. No crying. No heavy breathing. I wasn't even cursing; it was simply frayed nerves having complete sway over my being at that fully actualized moment.

So, fast-forwarding to yesterday afternoon, it all came back to me: Why hadn't I been killed twenty-two years ago? Why hadn't I died when I fell off a thirty-foot cliff overlooking Fine View Park in Pittsburgh when I was three years old? Why didn't I drown in that lake near Rhinelander, Wisconsin when I was seventeen... or when I got caught in deadly undertow while snorkeling in the Bahamas eight years later? Why did that double-decker bus in London not splatter me in 1984? And why hadn't I just been obliterated in a broad side accident just a few minutes earlier? Why hadn't I permanently maimed (or worse) that pedestrian just half a minute later?

Why is Life gracious to me? I don't believe much in fate or complete predestination... if I did, then ultimately, we would be nothing more than some sort of skin-covered robots. But I do sense divine providence. It's a mystery brimming with wonder. There *must* be more for me to do here. I should be thankful for every breath I have, making the most of the relationships and purposes that are enfolded into my life. That's what I choose to take from this fresh experience... this lesson... this reminder.

CHAPTER 3

BLACK SHEEP

No one has ever proven to me otherwise: I believe there is at least one black sheep in every family. Now don't think that means that because one family member turns out radically different than the rest of the flock, that it is necessarily a bad thing. But, more often than not, it does tend to cast a distinct shadow on everyone else.

James David Hollingsworth is my brother. Born two and a half years ahead of me, he was the first in our threesome of cubs. Likewise, my sis Joyce came two and a half years after me. Jim was a slight child, taking after Dad, who himself was quite thin even into his twenties. When he was just three, he was diagnosed with rickets, but in later years, we came to realize that assessment was wrong. Jim also suffered from asthma. But overall, he was a sweet little boy with a big smile and even bigger ears.

One of my favorite photos is of a three-year-old Jimmy hugging my fat little sixth-month-old punum. He was already skinnier than most children his age, and yet I was a plump Winston Churchill looking chap. It's funny how you can see so much personality in a toddler's face that carries into their later years. In that slightly out-of-focus Brownie Instamatic black and white shot, Jim's countenance is one of playfulness with his baby teeth proudly displayed and his arm firmly around the shoulder of his little bro with the double chin.

Living in smaller houses in Homer City and Pittsburgh, PA, Columbus, Ohio, and finally in Decatur, Illinois, meant that Jim and I were roommates all the way through high school. As little guys, we got along pretty well, with countless forays into variations on cops and robbers, combat, cowboys and injuns, chicken fights, and dirt clod wars. We built Lionel and H.O. train set-ups, made model planes, cars, and ships, and played wiffle ball and soccer for hours on end.

Jim took after my mother and was quite musically inclined. He played violin and was promoted to first chair in elementary, junior, and senior high orchestras. That acumen carried over into his love of guitar, which was stoked by the emergence of the Beatles. I can still remember that Sunday evening in early '64 when we were all gathered around the TV to watch *The Ed Sullivan Show* and their American debut. Like so many million others watching that night, things would never quite be the same. Within that next year, Jim was always the first on our block with the latest Beatles single (and subsequent albums), and he was quickly learning all the chords to their songs as well as other British Invasion bands that followed in the Fab Four's wake like the Stones, Dave Clark Five, and the Kinks.

It was during this period that Jim began defining himself in a way that was becoming increasingly counter to what Mom and Dad saw appropriate. He wanted a "Mop Top" haircut, and did whatever he could to make his coif look English. He lobbied hard for different types of shoes and clothes. These renegade appearances were an embarrassment for a preacher's family, and the tension was building from without as well as within. Jim became less interested in church activities and was becoming sullen and withdrawn in our family devotions. He would sit stonewall in our prayer times.

Like so many parents of that time, my folks had little idea of how to deal with this. It was one of the first times in American history that a younger generation was beginning to question their elders in a more rebellious sense. JFK's assassination in '63 left a deep scar on our psyches. World War II had been over for close to twenty years, and the frustration of the subsequent "Cold War" with the communist powers was beginning to show through. The build-up in Vietnam was beginning to irritate many. With the draft of young men into the military still on the table, it was becoming clearer that conflict with "those godless pinkos" was on the immediate horizon again. This was birthing a deep level of unacceptance of "the way things are" within the burgeoning generation who had all been born in the 10 years following the end of the Big War. These "Baby Boomers" were entering into their teenage years and were beginning to show their distrust of the status quo.

Add into this my parents' histories, and one can begin to see the perfect storm that was brewing in my brother's heart. You see, Dad and Mom had both been raised in alcoholic homes where their fathers had created tremendous uncertainty due to drinking escapades. In Dad's case, it eventually led to his parents splitting up, and it probably would've been for the best if that had happened with my Mom's folks. Out of these intense dysfunctional upbringings, they both ended up coming to Christ in their early twenties. The fundamentalist movement of the late 1940s helped frame answers and solutions to their chaotic backgrounds. The mindset of: "If you say and do the right things, God will watch out for you and give you the desires of your heart," was prevalent. And they modeled and taught us three kids that mantra. But that just didn't seem to work in the way Jim saw his world unfolding. Nor would it for Joyce and me as we matured.

With hard questions being openly stated in the pop and rock music of the mid-60s, and the answers of the establishment being so irrelevant to the reality that many young people were beginning to fear, that cycle began feeding on itself. Within a short three-year-span, an entire counter-culture was born. Musicians like Jefferson Airplane, MC5, Grateful Dead, and Moby Grape came on the scene... and Jim was always the hippest kid in the neighborhood with all the cool albums and magazines. By now he had a Sears electric guitar and a little amplifier. He started garage bands that learned all the latest tunes, and he began emulating the newest garb. When he was supposed to get his hair cut, he often refused, or would get it done a different way than the standard "butch" or "crew cut" of the time. When he was caught with cigarettes, it only emboldened him to try marijuana.

One morning, not long after his thirteenth birthday, we awoke in our Upper Arlington, Ohio home to find that Jim was gone, along with Mom's car. He had apparently been plotting a getaway for months and stole a few hundred dollars out of Dad's little "safe." As they were scurrying around the kitchen making calls and wondering where on earth he might've gone, they asked me if I had heard him mention anything. I pondered and said, "Well, he always seems to be talking about Haight Ashbury in San Francisco—maybe he's driving out that way."

Dad proceeded to call State Highway Patrols in several Mid-western states. Early the next day, we got a call from the police in Salina, Kansas. They had picked Jim up, not for unsafe driving, but because he just looked too young to be behind the wheel. Indeed, he was headed out to join up with Janis Joplin, Blue Cheer, Country Joe

MacDonald, and the like in that famed neighborhood by the Bay. He had driven over 900 miles before he was caught.

As the next several years unfolded, things continued to deteriorate. Jim became ever more insolent, disrespectful, rude, and crass. My folks tried everything from psychological testing, to one-on-one counseling, to family therapy, to lenience, to tough love, to extended groundings...you name it. No matter what they tried, Jim simply withdrew himself further and further from wanting to be under their supervision or participating in any way with family life. If they forced him to do things, he did it so grudgingly that everyone involved was miserable. And when they would punish him he either stared at them blankly or even laughed at them as the chastisement was being doled out.

Now, I know my Dad was a workaholic minister—this is fairly common among the clergy—often being more concerned with the needs of "the flock" and not being as aware of one's own family. I also know my Mom had some tough depression issues she was dealing with due to her horrible family background. But overall, I think they did a pretty good job of trying to raise a family during the turbulent '60s. And certainly just about every other family we knew of was going through similar trials with rebellious teens in that decade.

Being his roomie was interesting, to say the least. We shared a little hi-fi record player. He would play the latest Vanilla Fudge, then I would play some Rossini overture. He would respond by slapping on Frank Zappa and the Mothers of Invention, and I would follow-up with a Beethoven concerto. He would peel paint off the wall with Cream, and I'd play the Ben Hur soundtrack. He would spin the latest counter-culture comedy disc by Firesign Theater, and I would then offer Bill Cosby's *Why Is There Air?* Don't get me wrong, I liked a lot of what he played (many of those are still in my collection today).

Besides his edgy music tastes, he also had a truly sadistic streak that ran pretty deep. I remember once when he and I were on our bikes riding home from a junior high school activity. We stopped at the Sunoco station a few miles from our home to buy a couple of sodas. He studiously watched the service station attendant wash and squeegee the huge window on the front of the building. I kept asking him when we were gonna leave, but Jim said, "Just wait a little while." I thought perhaps he was interested in the careful technique the man employed... maybe Jim wanted to someday be a professional window washer or something. Anyway, after about ten minutes, the man stepped down off his ladder, put his hands on his hips and nodded at his handiwork.

Jim scootched forward on his bike, shook his can of Coke furiously, and then aimed it at the huge pane of glass as he peeled back the pop-top. A gusher of sticky pop went flying across the freshly cleansed surface, with the man standing just a dozen feet away. "C'mon!" Jim yelled as we began to furiously peddle away from the cursing employee. He laughed the whole way home.

He also liked to abuse neighborhood kids on Halloween by slashing their bike tires or hosing them down from a rooftop as they wandered by in their little Casper the Ghost and Johnny Qwest costumes. He would make elaborate life-like dummies and stage hangings in a tree as little ones would walk by, or he'd toss the "carcass" out into the dark street in front of cars cruising by.

On more than one occasion when he was left "in charge" while Mom and Dad were out running errands, Jim would chase Joyce and I around the house with a huge carving knife with us shrieking in mock (or was it?) terror. We knew he was kidding... but still, you have to admit that's pretty intense.

On top of those odd tendencies, I was becoming increasingly concerned about his use of narcotics. Mom and Dad were perturbed enough with his tobacco and weed, but they didn't realize he had graduated to needles. Heroin was his drug of choice during his junior and senior year. And he even began dealing in it. There were several months where I seriously considered turning him in because I was so deeply worried for his health—not only from bad trips, but also being mixed up with such a dangerous crowd of thugs.

In '69, we moved from the rolling hills of mid-Ohio to the flatlands of central Illinois where my Dad chose to pastor a church in Decatur. Perhaps this sleepy burg known as "The Soybean Capital of the World" would help steer my brother away from the cosmopolitan climes of Ohio's epicenter. It didn't work.

When I got excited about my faith during my sophomore year, Jim became more sarcastic toward me... thinking I was just trying to suck up to Mom and Dad's weird viewpoints on "gawd" and religion. He scoffed at some of the new "Jesus Rock" music I was listening to like Larry Norman, e band, and Wilson McKinley on our shared stereo. Jim had progressed into Zeppelin, Deep Purple, Savoy Brown, Allman Brothers, and Uriah Heep. I remember one night when he was stoned, he was dancing naked in front of his homemade strobe light while listening to King Crimson's "21st Century Schizoid Man" at concert volume. Quite the image, let me tell you.

By this point, Jim was regularly getting in trouble at school for cutting classes, taunting teachers, getting caught smoking, inappropriate attire (he loved to attach the American flag into the seat of his pants, or embroider certain lovely phrases into his blue jean jacket, or bell bottom jeans with dozens of little bells sewn into the decorative cuff that disrupted everyone as he would walk).

Even though academics slipped far down his list of priorities, he applied himself strongly toward his efforts with his guitar. The bands he helped form were becoming pretty well known locally, and they even went to neighboring towns for gigs. On a few occasions, they opened some shows and became friends with one of the area's cool bands that got signed a year later: R.E.O. Speedwagon.

Jim's eighteenth birthday fell almost exactly on his graduation. He had been jonesing for months about his ultimate escape from the grip of my folks. When I would ask him what he planned on doing once he was out, he would just sneer and tell me "anything to get away from this insane asylum."

I'll never forget that final day. We all returned from the graduation ceremony, and he bolted for our basement bedroom where he had everything packed-up and ready to go. Some of his reefer head buddies came in a pickup truck to meet him, and within ten minutes, they loaded up all his earthly possessions as we stood and watched. I hadn't seen Jim move that fast in years. My folks, Joyce, and I were somewhat speechless about how quickly he was bugging out.

With two big boxes in his arms, he backed his way through the screen door leading out to the side driveway for the final time. With all of us standing there, he paused. Maybe he would say something halfway nice on his farewell. He stared at all of us, and then, measuring his words carefully he declared, "You guys are all fuckin' nuts... and I don't ever want to see any of you again. Good riddance."

The screen door slammed. "Let's get out of here!" he roared as he jumped into the back of the truck, which spewed gravel as they tore out of the driveway.

We kind of stood there dumbstruck. Mom looked over at Dad and started to cry. As I recall, she sobbed quite a bit over Jim for many years afterwards. Joyce and I shrugged our shoulders as if to say, "Well, now *that* is over with."

CHAPTER 4

FLOCKS IN FLUX

After Jim's turbulent final years in our home—and his acidic "farewell"—things calmed down quite a bit within the Hollingsworth household. I was getting more involved in sports, and I became more deeply excited about my faith in Christ due to the Jesus People that came to Decatur every summer in the early '70s. This group of itinerant hippies that had been radically saved set up a large circus tent on a vacant lot they would rent, and they'd pack it out every evening with rallies that featured a heavy blues rock band and preaching from a wild-haired Pentecostal minister turned evangelist. It became the "in" place to be, and that tent was packed with close to a thousand people every night. Usually hundreds came forward each evening after the concert/sermon combo to receive the gift of faith. By 1972, it seemed like at least half of the teenagers in that city of 100,000 had come to know Christ in this very relevant way.

There was a real hunger to grow spiritually, so there were Bible studies springing up in all the local high schools. Churches that were open to what was happening had youth groups that were booming. To his credit, my Dad was very accepting toward all these kids looking for a shepherd, even though he took some heat from more conservative members of his staid Presbyterian flock. At one point we probably had nearly a hundred teens in our group, many of the unkempt longhaired variety. Woodland Chapel became the primary home for spiritual growth for lots of kids on our side of Lake Decatur.

We started our own Christian rock band called Maranatha. Actually, it included a rather sizeable "choir," with all sorts of percussion, including the ever-present tambourines (what *were* we thinking?)... so it was more of some sort of "rock ensemble," I guess. We weren't very good, especially with me on drums, but it was a great outlet for our energy and enthusiasm. I also plunked around in another band we gave the brilliant moniker of International Harvester (kinda clever for some teenagers from corn country), but I don't recall us ever actually playing a gig.

After my graduation, I began my collegiate career at Wheaton College. Bringing my excitement for Jesus through germane music with me, I quickly became immersed with promoting Christian rock concerts on and off campus, writing a music column for the student paper, DJ'ing at the campus radio station, etc. This lead to me starting my own booking agency during my sophomore year, called Rock of Ages, which set up concerts for nineteen artists including Love Song, Randy Matthews, Larry Norman, Resurrection Band, and Randy Stonehill among others. I also began writing for national music publications—both mainstream and Christian—from *Walrus* to *Harmony*, from *Triad* to *Billboard*, from *Cash Box* to *Christianity Today*.

I guess because I was around Jim in those developing years, I felt comfortable hanging with rock musicians. Here I was, a somewhat sheltered church kid from a small Midwest town interviewing Black Sabbath, Boston, Genesis, Van Halen, ELO, The Tubes, Charlie

Daniels, Ambrosia, Stanley Clark, Jeff Beck, Yes, Peter Gabriel, Rush, Atlanta Rhythm Section, Styx, and many others while I was still a teenager. If you saw Cameron Crowe's *Almost Famous*, it was essentially my story as well (although I didn't lose my virginity to a harem of groupies in a Greenville, Tennessee motel room).

True to his word, my brother was quite incommunicado during this whole stretch—over three full years after his high school graduation. We had heard rumors he was in Quebec trying to avoid the draft (false), living in a hippie commune in the Smokies (false), part of a band in New Orleans (partially true), and out west somewhere near the Grand Canyon (true). It also turned out that he had been living just twenty-five miles away from us in a farmhouse with some other weed heads for about half of that time.

I actually stumbled upon him quite by accident while I was on a painting job during summer break from college. While thirty feet up applying trim on some gutters, I heard a voice that sounded very much like my brother's coming from the neighbor's yard below me. I turned around as best I could without dropping my can of Sherwin Williams to see Jim, with his hair halfway down to his back, a huge handlebar mustache, and mirrored shades getting an amp out of a beat-up Pontiac Firebird.

"Hey, Jim!" I yelled. He looked around kind of befuddled, and I repeated myself.

He realized he was being beckoned from above and looked up. "Oh... hi, Mark," he said nonchalantly as if we had just spoken yesterday. He had to have been one of the most laid-back dudes in history.

I nearly slid down the ladder, I was so anxious to see him. We caught up for a bit, and I learned he had been following his dream of playing professionally in rock bands. He certainly wasn't getting rich, but he seemed to be enjoying it. I got his address and phone number, and I reminded him of ours. Mom and Dad were excited to finally know where he was, and they invited him over, but he didn't take them up on it.

About a month later, though, he did come to our Grandpa's funeral. We were all very kind toward him, and he seemed to be in a decent attitude. But it wasn't until his rented ramshackle house burned down in the middle of a frigid January evening that we heard from him again. He called out of desperation and Mom and Dad gladly took him in until he could find a new place. Later that winter, he ended up catching pneumonia, and they once again housed him and paid for his medical bills while he recovered at their home.

I came home from college to see him both times, and we roomed together like in the old days. He was nearly a walking skeleton from lousy eating habits and even more doltish drug intake. The needle marks and bandages in his arms and behind his knees were numerous, but he hid them from my parents by always wearing long-sleeved shirts and pants. We all did our best to make him feel welcome, but he treated it more like an inconvenience. He never thanked my parents for their help.

When Jim saw that I was pretty involved with all this music business, he was somewhat curious but always scoffed at the "gawd rawk," as he liked to call it.

In early '75, my Dad decided to transfer to a church in the Chicago area. The only time we spoke with Jim back in central Illinois was when we initiated it. He did come to visit once on Turkey Day several years later, and we had a great time talking about rock'n'roll. I had certainly grown in my knowledge of "the biz," and we had a good respect going for each other when talking about the latest trends. It turns out we both liked a lot of the same bands by this point, and it was good to feel some camaraderie with him about at least that. One memory of that visit was our busting out in laughter listening to Steve Martin's *Let's Get Small* album.

But for the most part, he kept to himself despite our calls, letters, and cards. Whenever I would go back to Decatur to visit old friends, I would try to see him, but usually with little success. I guess I didn't realize that this treadmill was taking its toll on my spirit. My reserves were running low and about to reach a critical point.

CHAPTER 5

DECLARATION OF SEPARATION

Don't kid yourself
And don't fool yourself
This love's too good to last
And I'm too old to dream

(Muse, "Blackout" from *Absolution*, 2004)

"I've decided that I'm no longer a Christian," I matter-of-factly stated in between bites of my processed meatloaf. It was lunchtime in the busy Wheaton College dining hall, and my buddies J.R., Randy, and Chuck weren't quite sure they heard me.

"What was that?" asked Julie, another pal who was sitting across from me. The clatter of cutlery on china, tinkling glass, and dull roar of hundreds of conversant collegians made it hard to hear... but what I said seemingly came out of the blue, and it wasn't a normal statement made by a junior at Billy Graham's alma mater.

"I've really been thinking about it, and I just don't think a relationship with Christ makes sense to me anymore," I explained. They all started to chuckle, knowing that I was a clown and often made farcical commentary just to raise eyebrows. They leaned forward wondering what kind of punch line was coming to my joke. I sat there silent. After a long pause while stirring my syrupy mashed potatoes, I punctuated with a firm: "I'm as serious as a God damn heart attack."

Now I fully had everyone's attention.

"Mark, we know things have been tough lately, but c'mon, it can't be that hard," Chuck implored.

"Well, from everything I've experienced these past couple of months, it seems like God just doesn't care... or maybe He's incapable of making a difference in many of our lives." I took a long sip of my ice tea. J.R. slid back. Randy averted his gaze. Julie scrutinized me. Chuck was shaking his head slowly... almost in disbelief.

He and I had gone through a lot as best friends in high school. He had lost his Dad to cancer the year before I moved to Decatur, and we became nearly inseparable buds from our first year of high school onward. Both of us had come to a deep level of committed faith during that time, and we each decided to continue our quest together at Wheaton. We were roommates our freshman and sophomore years there and continued to hang out regularly.

Chuck and the others knew that I had recently been hurt by my relationship not working out with Lisa the way I had hoped. It was the first time I had really had my heart broken, and seeing her regularly around the small campus did nothing to help me get past my sadness.

They also knew I had been struggling with some probing questions about the canon of scripture (how the New Testament as we know it was basically voted on by a bunch of scholars about 350 years after Christ's life on earth). Who were they to choose what was God's Word? And how could any of it be considered error-free when it was written by dozens of different flawed humans over an 800-year period? I was likewise wrestling with the concept of free will vs. predestination among other theological conundrums. And, of course, there were all the weighty concerns about Jim and how he had sabotaged our family.

But just as the more mature Freud determined that mankind's deep insecurities were defined by our fear of death (as opposed to the basic human longing for sex in his earlier teachings), I was staring deep into a chasm of doubt about my finite existence.

Even in the quietest moments
I wish I knew
What I had to do
And even though the sun is shining
Well I feel the rain
Here it comes again
(Supertramp, "Even In The Quietest Moments" from album by same name, 1977)

You see, there were three other friends I had helped lead to Jesus while in high school. Ernie was the stereotypical stoner: rebellious, aloof, a wisenheimer, and a lot brighter than he liked to let on. His long golden hair was parted on the side, and he loved to flip it out of his eyes to accentuate his points. John was a quiet soul and a pretty good athlete in our pick-up games of baseball, basketball, and football. Even before he could drive, he got into cars and really knew his way around the underside of a hood. Mike was a handsome kid and was part of the "socialite" crowd, which gave him a lot of stroke in just about any area he chose. But each of them came to faith during our sophomore years, eagerly diving into the scriptures and boldly carrying their Bibles to school each day. We had so many good discussions about where God was leading each of us, and we were all striving to grow in our young faith.

However, over the next few years, their resolve wavered in various ways. Ernie's home life was not going well due to his parents' divorce, and he escaped back into drugging. John got more and more enamored with the whole motor head crowd and was going out drinking several nights a week. Mike got pulled back in with "the beautiful people" and lost interest in being a disciple.

Most of my Christian friends decided it was best to shun these guys. Maybe they were afraid that they would "backslide" too if they hung out with them, so they were rattled to be in their proximity. But unfortunately, their avoidance came across much more like judging. I guess because my brother had been such a wayward soul in those years, I had no fear of staying in touch with these three. So I would continue to befriend them in and around school (if they didn't think I was messing with their particular subculture), or go out riding, and goof around at times at our homes, or movies, or what-have-you on weekends.

Even when I went off to college, I stayed in touch with them via letters, calls, and I'd look them up when I would return to central Illinois on breaks. If they wanted to meet at a bar, I would do it. Over those three years or so, we had some poignant heart-to-heart talks. I knew they were bummed about some choices they had made. And I knew that a portion of that pain had been compounded by holier-than-thou Christians looking down their noses at them. I told them not to worry about jerks like that. But, of course, it was a helpful tool in their box of excuses and rationalizations why they didn't want to follow Jesus anymore.

On one hand, their falling away helped give me some sense of mission in my life, and I truly wanted the best for them. Equally, however, it chafed at my spirit... I hurt for them the same way I hurt for Jim. "Why are you allowing this to happen, God? Will you please

intercede... please help soften their hardened hearts?" I often questioned.

Nowhere in the corridors of pale green and gray
Nowhere in the suburbs
In the cold light of day
There in the midst of it so alive and alone
Words support like bone

Dreaming of mercy street
Wear your inside out
Dreaming of mercy
'Swear they moved that sign
Dreaming of mercy
In your daddy's arms

(Peter Gabriel, "Mercy Street," from *So*, 1986)

All of this was piling up concurrent with the other doubts I
mentioned earlier. I was becoming tenser in my interactions with
Christians and more hesitant with God. Even though I was striving
to serve through Bible studies, counseling at a coffeehouse, tutoring
in the inner city, and booking/promoting Christian concerts, I was
simultaneously wondering what the point of it all was. So I shared
this openly with my close circle of friends, and they tried their best
to reassure me. But they didn't have any satisfactory answers, and
they were growing concerned with my irritability.

Then, right after Christmas break of my junior year at Wheaton,
it all started to unravel. In a six week period, each of those three
guys died. Ernie overdosed on heroin, most likely on purpose. John
got stinkin' drunk again and was shredded when he flew through

his windshield as his car collided with a tree. Mike was stoned at a party and fell out of a third story window, snapping his neck and back on contact with the cement below.

For the first two, I found rides down to Decatur to try to help console loved ones and friends. But my depression was darker than the Black Canyon on a moonless night. Then when I heard about Mike, I couldn't bear to go again.

We turn away to face the cold, enduring chill
As the day begs the night for mercy love
The sun so bright it leaves no shadows
Only scars carved into stone
On the face of earth
The moon is up and over One Tree Hill
We see the sun go down in your eyes
(U2, "One Tree Hill" from *The Joshua Tree,* 1987)

So there I was, sitting in the Wheaton cafeteria. I hadn't slept much in the three previous nights since the final call. I thoroughly searched my will and came to the conclusion that this simply wasn't acceptable anymore. I wasn't necessarily mad at God, although I certainly had some blistering questions. It was more that it just didn't seem to make sense... for me anyway. Maybe it did for all these other confident, young evangelicals... for these fundies who never questioned anything. Maybe even for some who truly had walked through some horrifying experiences like some transfers from the Congo or missionary kids I knew who had been through stark experiences in Bangladesh and Chile.

But for me, I couldn't relate any further. It just wasn't adding up. My once stout faith was now fragile... even crumbling. And no thing or no one seemed to be able to give me any respite from the anguish in the harsh light of day, let alone the dark night of the soul.

As the next few months unfolded, I found myself in a quite unique position: an active non-Christian at the college whose slogan was: "For Christ and His Kingdom."

I can't light no more of your darkness
All my pictures seem to fade to black and white
I'm growing tired and time stands still before me
Frozen here on the ladder of my life

(Elton John, "Don't Let the Sun Go Down On Me," from *Caribou*, 1974)

CHAPTER 6

DARKNESS AROUND
AND WITHIN

Blackbird singing in the dead of night
Take these sunken eyes and learn to see
All your life you were only waiting
For this moment to be free

Blackbird fly, Blackbird fly
Into the light of the dark black night
(The Beatles, "Blackbird" from *The White Album,* 1968)

As the days rolled into weeks, then into months, my anguish over the loss of Ernie, John, and Mike continued. Eventually it morphed into a level of depression... even bitterness. Another Wheaton buddy of mine, Malcolm, was going through severe questioning as well, and we shared many lengthy conversations. In some ways, we felt like we were breaking free from preordained expectations that others had put on us as "dynamic young evangelical leaders"... you know, Wheaton's reputation for that sort of thing known across Christendom and all. We knew what we were flying from, but little idea of where we were headed.

Now, don't get me wrong... I didn't suddenly go on some hellacious quest for out-of-control binge drinking, or bonging like a Dead head, or soliciting whores, or attempting to burn down 140 year-old Blanchard Hall (the Holy of Holies).

About the only thing that started to distinctly manifest itself outwardly was my newfound coarse language. I had never sworn in my life up until that point. The crudest thing I would say was "crap," and I always meant it in reference to the stuff that was caked on the bottom of a garbage can. But as soon as I decided to no longer hoist the Christian banner, the foul invective began to flow out of me like Vesuvius on Pompeii. When something struck me the right way, I could turn out a combination of verbs and descriptive accoutrement that would make even the bluest sailor blush. I would get plenty of strange looks from fellow students and even the occasional tongue wagging from one who was up for the challenge of reprimanding me. But most people seemed to know it was best to steer clear.

Lack of consistent sleep, and all the non-stop reminders that a religious surrounding can supply, weighed heavily. All the repetitive God talk and sunny Christian platitudes only served to darken my mood. And when I would ponder deep mysteries about "God's will" and where my friends were after their deaths, I felt that they and I were definitely getting the short end of the stick. *Why does God create free will if He knows we're going to be weak and sin in the first place, thus always falling short of His righteousness? It seems like we're doomed to make the wrong choices even before we're born.*

From the depths of a hooded nightmare, I saw what could not be
Mysteries and mayhem from the pinnacle I see

There's no answer when there's no question

The mark of Cain bears hard on me

(Kansas, "Mysteries and Mayhem" from *Masque*, 1975)

By the time spring break came along, I decided to take at least six months off. I looked hard at finishing my degree at a state school. Unfortunately, I had taken so many Bible, Christian Education, and ancient Greek courses that only about half of my credits would transfer to a secular university, effectively knocking me back to being a second semester sophomore. I couldn't bear the idea of adding on another two years of college. I was nearly a senior, and I just wanted to get it over with. So, with some trepidation, I decided to go ahead and finish out at Wheaton, even though I no longer believed the core values there.

How can I believe

When I don't trust?

All your theories

Turn to dust

(Muse, "City of Delusion" from *Black Holes and Revelations*, 2006)

It was my desire to be as forthright as possible with my fellow students and professors about what I was going through. I figured there was no point whatsoever in pussyfooting around. So I would bring up tough questions in my classes. I would argue with smug young right-wingers (of which there was an overabundance at Wheaton). I would publicly criticize hypocrisy in school policies. I wrote interesting articles in the campus paper that stirred the ire of some.

I stood up in the middle of a chapel service and told a missionary representative who was pleading for donations in front of 2,200 fellow students that he was "so full of shit" and walked out of the meeting (sadly for him I had seen him pull up behind the building thirty minutes before in a brand new Mercedes).

For my senior dissertation, my fellow Speech majors and I were asked to write a detailed paper on "The Theory of Christian Communication." I entitled mine "Why Christian Communication is Bullshit." Much to my professor's credit, he actually gave me a B+ for stating my case convincingly.

Double faces dark defense
Talk too loud but talk no sense
Yeah I see those smiling eyes
Butter us up with smiling lies

(Emerson, Lake, and Palmer, "The Curse of Baba Yaga" from *Pictures at an Exhibition*, 1971)

Of course, some of these activities got me in hot water with the administration, and I was called on the carpet on several occasions for being a disruptive force. But I would always give impassioned and informed arguments, and once more, to their merit, they didn't expel me. The chaplain and I even had some good talks, and I am grateful to this day for his openness and concern over my torment.

There were some other students who stuck by me, too. I'll always have a soft spot for that handful that would entertain my venting, would listen long, and would even challenge me lovingly.

I suppose if I had to label myself at that point, I was an antagonized agnostic. I still felt that God was there. In fact, I still believed in the Christ. We just weren't connecting anymore... I dunno... maybe it was a mutual alienation. And much of the religious sub-culture only exacerbated my raw wounds. Prayer was either an irritant or an empty exercise. In fact, I looked through my prayer journal from my early years at Wheaton, and I realized that so many situations I had interceded about had been unanswered or had turned out pretty much the opposite of what would've seemed like the best result.

I felt I needed to do some serious research within other mindsets to get a better grip on what it was that I did and did not believe. Due to my heavy class load, working several part time jobs to help pay the tuition, and my side avocations in radio and music journalism, there was little time for comparative thinking. I began to keep a list of people and philosophies I wanted to check into once the collegiate merry-go-round was finished. I just knew that I needed to finish well on my Speech Communication degree if I was to make any headway in the rock radio field after graduation.

You see, music had firmly taken root in me, and it was not only my plan as a career—it had become my lifeline. To what it was exactly tethered, I wasn't sure... but as someone once said, "Music is what feelings sound like," and I needed that consolation. It helped bring resonance to my pain and fueled my determination to face it head on. And it would play a huge part in bringing about resolve as time moved along.

Inside a window that leads to your conscience you'll see, you'll hear
People are talking, maybe you know them, they know you're near
Masking themselves from fear
And asking themselves who their friends are
Save me for now, save me forever
Hold me so close, I can't bear to go
There's darkness around me or is it within me?
You're living forever, I'm dying so slow
(Kansas, "Angels Have Fallen," from *Monolith,* 1979)

CHAPTER 7

ENACTING THE MASQUE

Each man has a memory
Much more than the eye can see
Yet still others linger deep inside you
Haunting thoughts of pain and joy divide you
Look beyond your eyes
At the dark and moody skies
For they're standing in your way
You must find the light of day

(Kansas, "Apercu," from *Kansas,* 1974)

I'll never forget that warm Indian summer evening when I would be introduced to something that would ultimately impact my life in many ways. It was sixteen months before my decision to renounce my faith, and I was playing sand volleyball next to one of the dormitories at Wheaton College. Four stories above us, a student had placed both of his huge Jensen speakers against his window and began blasting some of the most stimulating music I'd heard in a long time. Asking several in our group if they had any idea who it was, we all became curious.

When we were finished, I climbed the stairs and sauntered down the hallway to the door of the room from where the music was emanating. I had to knock several times in order to be heard over the symphonic rock of intricate drum patterns, blistering guitars, crisp keyboard riffs, and soaring vocals. But what set it apart from other great bands of that time like Yes, Queen, and ELP, was the distinctive use of violin as a rock instrument.

When a scruffy-faced kid with a shoulder length mane opened the door, the massive sound was made all the clearer. So as not to make him feel like I was some goody-two-shoes there to complain about his "jungle rhythm heathen rawk," I extended my hand and yelled, "My name's Mark. What on earth is this great music you're playing?"

"Cool... I'm Rich. You dig it?! It's a band called Kansas." He handed me the cover, and I recognized it from the local record store racks. You see, I frequented Johnny B.Goode—a music and head shop in downtown Wheaton—at least once a week to check out new releases. The proprietor, Don McLeese, eventually went on to become a pretty well-known syndicated music journalist for the *Chicago Sun Times*. He'd often play hip new stuff, and it helped in my quest to stay on top of all the latest trends. Earlier that spring, I had seen this same album in the New Releases Bin, but because of the band's appearance, of plaid shirts, ripped jeans, and even one of the dudes wearing bib overalls, I presumed they were some sort of country bumpkin git-fiddle band a la Charlie Daniels. Man, was I wrong.

I asked Rich if I could listen for a while, and he eagerly complied by offering me a beanbag chair and lifting the needle to start the record from the beginning. "Check out the lyrics, too... pretty amazing stuff."

From the very start
I screamed for the devil to let me be
I called to the heavens to set me free
Today I prayed for the answer and not one
Of your gods in the sky would rescue me

(Kansas, "Journey From Mariabronne," from *Kansas*, 1974)

It was breathtaking to hear something that so immediately captured my imagination. As a kid, I had always loved the romantic era of classical music, and then as the rock explosion of the mid-to-late '60s came along I was swept up into that, with my brother's help. And even though the progressive rock scene started to meld the two with some powerful bands like those mentioned above, there was still something missing. I was now hearing it, and it was mesmerizing. Incorporating elements of Hendrix, Deep Purple, Zeppelin, Mahavishnu, and even Leo Kottke—with powerful arrangements and orchestrations influenced by the likes of Mahler, Wagner, Debussy, and Tchaikovsky—was the perfect blend of power and serenity. To top it off, the lyrics were at times probing, then confessional. Some angry... others contemplative. But there was honesty and yearning to it all, and when mixed with the music, it made a delicious feast.

The next day I promptly bought their first two releases. I tried finding out everything I could about this obscure band from Topeka that was really beginning to make noise across the country. I became especially taken with the songs by guitarist/keyboardist Kerry Livgren. He seemed the more classically inspired of the composers, and I resonated deeply with much of what he spoke. I couldn't help but begin praying regularly for such an ardent seeker.

Run a silent path to nowhere, everything is all
You could have a pleasant life if Summer had no Fall

Treat yourself so gently though the task is often hard
Man is not a God it seems, who holds the final card
Close your eyes and feel the darkness, speak and hear the sound
We only catch a glimpse of all the life that is around
The man is not alive who knows the value of his soul
And when our lives are pulled away, there's more to fill the hole
I wonder what you'd think if all the changes didn't come?

(Kansas, "Incommudro," from *Song For America*, 1975)

As my misgivings about elements of Christianity were becoming more defined, I found Kerry's words giving me solace... even giving me strength to keep moving forward in my search for clarity.

A few months later, I was the first at Wheaton to get their third album, entitled *Masque*. A French word that means, "A disguise of reality created through a theatrical or musical performance." So much of what I was struggling with was reflected in the album art: Arcimboldo's eerie *Water*. It was a surrealist painting of a native warlord's head that on closer examination was actually a conglomeration of aquatic creatures and plants writhing about. This is how I often felt... From a distance, I was one who could somehow fit in, but in reality, there was a complex, even squeamish jumble of questions that made me—and others—feel uneasy.

With glory and passion no longer in fashion
The hero breaks his blade
Cast this shadow long that I may hide my face
And in this cloak of darkness the world I will embrace
In all that I endure, of one thing I am sure
Knowledge and reason change like the season
A jester's promenade

(Kansas, "The Pinnacle," from *Masque*, 1975)

So during my junior year, during the six-week stretch in which my three friends perished, I finally saw Kansas perform twice. In their first three years of national exposure, Kansas had become known as "the touringest band in the land," averaging close to 250 concerts per year. They opened for seemingly anyone and everyone, and they played around Chicagoland alone eleven times that year. They were also gaining quite the reputation as a band that many did not want to have on the same bill because they regularly blew others off the stage with their force and skill. For instance, at a recent gig as opener for Rory Gallagher at the infamous Aragon Ballroom, most of the sold out audience left during the Irishman's set, having been so thoroughly entertained by the sextet from the desolate heartland.

Despite the lack of a hit single, each album was selling more than the one before, and Kansas was beginning to garner headline gigs at universities and in major cities.

It was hard to imagine a group being able to pull off the intricate arrangements of their complex epics... but they did so even more convincingly on stage than on their albums. The music was more primal and urgent in person, and with creative lighting and theatrical staging to help interpret the many moods, the concerts were everything I had hoped. In fact, at the show at College of DuPage, I met up with Doug Pinnick, the lead singer/bassist for an area hard rock outfit I'd gotten to know (and now famous with King's X). Kansas was also his favorite band, and we were enthralled with what we experienced.

"Man, Kerry Livgren is so far into my head now. He seems to be writing for me," declared Doug, who had also experienced deep grief and spiritual anxiety growing up. And with what I had been going through with my heavy losses, I had to concur.

Sweet child of innocence

Living in the present tense

Father Time will take his toll

Rack your body and steal your soul

What became of all the years?

Are you drowning in your tears?

Who will catch you when you fall?

Who will hear you when you call?

(Kansas, "Child of Innocence," from *Masque*, 1975)

The leading monthly music paper in Chitown, *The Illinois Enter-tainer*, asked if I would like to become a regular contributor after seeing some of my other rock journalism. One of the first assign-ments I requested was to interview Kansas.

The band had just put the finishing touches on their *Leftover-ture* album, and they were doing a quick run of dates across the Midwest to help pay some bills before the album would be released a few months later. Kansas' popularity had grown to beyond cult status in Chicago by that point, and the small Randhurst Ice Arena in suburban Palatine was packed with 4,000 "wheatheads."

In a dingy, dripping, rackety locker room (abundant with the stench of sweat-soaked leather padding that hockey players are known for), I met Kerry Livgren for the first time, while the Earl Slick Band pounded out senseless drivel to the impatient masses sitting above us. It remains one of my favorite interviews ever, par-tially because Kerry was excited to be answering intelligent ques-tions about his band's music from someone who had done his homework, but also because we really started to hit it off. In the forty-minute session, we learned that we loved many of the same classical composers, knew way more than we would normally ad-mit about detasseling corn; were influenced by many of the same writers, philosophers, and filmmakers; shared in deep-seeded distrust of the music business, could both quote Monty Python ad infinitum... and were both on a quest for truth and meaning that was paramount above all else.

I felt so comfortable with him, that at one point, I asked if he were ever open to suggestions for their set. "Normally not, but you're more interesting than the average bear, so go ahead." I told him that I'd always been fond of Franz Liszt ("Me, too" he interjected), and his Hungarian Rhapsody series ("Once again, me as well," he chimed).

"Have you ever thought about adapting one of those pieces somewhere in your set? They are so fun; Robbie (Steinhardt—the band violinist) could easily pull it off, and I'm sure your crowds would love it."

Knowing that this was their first gig on this run of dates and that everything they would be playing that night would be new to me, Kerry sat there amazed. "Well, as a matter of fact, we ARE playing a bit of one of Liszt's pieces during the encore."

At that point, my photographer, Sam Smith, said, "This is just too strange with you two."

"Yeah," Kerry concurred, "It's like we're two long lost brothers or something."

We agreed to chat more after the show (Kerry really wanted us to see the cover art from the new album). We headed out into the packed arena, and we weaseled our way down to about fifteen feet in front of the stage into the general admission floor "seating." I have seen over 2,000 musical performances in my life, and what I was about to experience would be one of the tops on that list.

Chapter 8

Encountering the Wall

hat followed was an amazing set I doubt that anyone in that crowd will ever forget. Kansas played many of their faithful's faves from the first three albums, plus every song from their yet-to-be-released classic *Leftoverture*. We experienced an inaugural peek into history. That piece has gone on to sell over 10 million units, and we were the ones hearing it performed live for the first time.

Opening with iconoclastic a capella harmonies of "Carry On Wayward Son," we all knew something very special was unfolding before us. Once again, Kerry's lyric went straight to where I was in wrestling with God:

> *Masquerading as a man with a reason*
> *My charade is the event of the season*
> *And if I claim to be a wise man*
> *It surely means that I don't know*
> *On a stormy sea of moving emotion*
> *Tossed about I'm like a ship on the ocean*
>
> (Kansas, "Carry On Wayward Son," from *Leftoverture*, 1976)

Each debut of a new song was greeted with enthusiasm. The band was plenty into the proceedings as well, visibly charged by the new material and the reaction it was receiving. During the sweeping guitar solo at the end of the lofty "Miracles Out of Nowhere," the tears were streaming down Livgren's face, playing as if his life were in the balance.

When we had been speaking beforehand, I'd asked Kerry what was the most meaningful lyric he had written. "One of the songs on the new album, 'The Wall' summarizes the search better than anything else. 'The Wall' says it all," he said with a knowing chuckle. When they played it, the urgency was palpable.

> *I'm woven in a fantasy, I can't believe the things I see*
> *The path that I have chosen now has led me to a wall*
> *And with each passing day I feel a little*
> *more like something dear was lost*
> *It rises now before me, a dark and silent barrier between*
> *All I am, and all that I would ever want be*
> *It's just a travesty, towering, marking*
> *off the boundaries my spirit would erase*
> *It's standing there, the symbol and the sum of all that's me*
> *It's just a travesty, towering,*
> *Blocking out the light and blinding me*
> *I want to see*
> (Kansas, "The Wall," from *Leftoverture*, 1976)

Sure enough, during the second encore, they did play a rousing version of "Hungarian Rhapsody #2" with great jest and fanfare in between "Song For America" and "Cheyenne Anthem." My buddy Sam and I couldn't stop laughing about my premonition.

After the show, I got to meet the rest of the band, and Kerry excitedly showed us a copy of the now-infamous album cover art for *Leftoverture*, featuring the DaVinci-like character pondering his muse.

Kerry and I exchanged contact info, and within weeks we were writing and calling regularly. Whenever Kansas was near Chicago, he would get me passes to come see him. Most times after the set, we would talk long into the night, sometimes until dawn, about all things musical, theatrical, philosophical, and spiritual. On one tour, I finally got to meet his sparkling wife, Vicci, whom he would always speak so fondly about. She was very down-to-earth and vivacious about life as well.

Because I had been so involved with Christian rock, I still had some affection for several artists whom I thought Kerry would enjoy. I figured that because of his longing for the transcendent, that he would be open to anyone who was seeking as well. So I gave him albums by Phil Keaggy, Petra, and 2nd Chapter of Acts— three artists whom I had done booking for and with whom I was still friends. Kerry got back in touch with me soon thereafter saying he enjoyed them. He, in turn, kept me abreast of cool new music like PFM, Kayak, and the Electromagnets (featuring a then-unknown guitar phenom by the name of Eric Johnson).

Over the next three years, Kerry and I communicated often. He invited me to his home in Atlanta, asked me to come to their platinum party for *Point of Know Return*, and he allowed me to sit in on some Kansas rehearsals and recording sessions. I got to know the rest of the band and their management as well from attending over two dozen shows.

In the center of our friendship was our communal search for meaning. Because he had been raised Lutheran and I was the son of a Presbyterian minister, we could certainly explore the scriptures and even the Apocrypha. But Kerry had been drawn toward the

Thanks for your support of my first book, *Embracing the Gray.*

Would you be willing to do me a big favor? If you enjoy the book, would you do me the honor of writing a Five Star Review at Amazon.com? As you may be aware, 80% of all books are now purchased via Amazon, and the reviews of readers carry more weight than mass media opinions. And Five Star reviews are the most read.

Go to Amazon.com and type "Embracing the Gray" in the search bar near the top of the page. The link should take you to the results page, where my book should be the first one listed. Click on that title, and it will take you to the full *Embracing the Gray* page. Then scroll down to Customer Reviews and click on "Create Your Own Review." Have some fun! You can write as long a piece as you like.

If you would also like to post the same review at BarnesAndNoble.com, BooksAMillion.com, Borders.com, Powells.com, etc, that would be great!

Once again, I really appreciate your support. Thanks for taking the time to help in this way.

Cheers,

mystics from the Far East, having been fascinated with Hinduism and Buddhism in particular—and various hybrids that he would dream up.

Since I was intrigued as well, I read *The Book of Tao*, the *Bhaga-vad-Gita*, *The Teachings of Confucius*, *The Koran*, and *The Book of Mormon*. I also studied the Stoics, Unitarians, Determinists, Materi-alists, Hedonists, Relativists, Utilitarianists, Socialists, Rationalists, Skeptics, and Empiricists (and probably ended up with cysts on my brain as a result!). I delved into philosophers like Akhenaton, Zoro-aster, Gandhi, Descartes, Mortimer J. Adler, Cicero, Sri Chimnoy, Vol-taire, Plato, Edmund Burke, Loa-Tse, Ayn Rand, Socrates, Hermann Hesse, Joseph Campbell, Nietzsche, Kierkegaard, Bertrand Russell, and Eric Fromme. I re-examined Christian mystics and thinkers like St. Augustine, Francis of Assisi, Tomas A. Kempis, John Bunyan, Martin Luther, and Francis Schaeffer. These all added greatly to our spirited communiqués, phone calls, and backstage discussions.

But it wasn't just Kerry who was prodding me forward. The primary catalysts included being free from Wheaton and out living on my own for the first time. My worldview was widening as I was mostly surrounded by people in the radio and music business that had little interest in matters of Christianity. In fact, most of them had little desire for anything except getting stoned or laid... but I did find some who liked to engage in deeper discussion. When others were out partying, I would often be holed-up somewhere reading or contemplating all of this stuff. And some of my college chums— who weren't intimidated by lively candor—continued to interact.

I'm on fire
Burning with the questions in my mind
Strange desire
Seems there's nothing else for me to find

'Cause I've been here, and I've been there

Seems like I've been everywhere before

I've seen it all a hundred times

Still I think there surely must be more

I've been livin'

I had to take my time and change my style

Now I wonder

Is something gonna make it all worthwhile?

I know there's more than meets the eye

Would like to see it before I die for sure

Something tells me it's all right

Only one step farther to the door

(Kansas, "Paradox," from *Point of Know Return*, 1977)

All of this head input gave me some assistance in processing the loss of Ernie, John, and Mike. But during those first few years out of the university, several more passed away: Charles, one of my college buds, died quickly from leukemia; Brian was killed in a car crash; Frankie, a Viet Nam vet from one of my Dad's old churches, committed suicide; my Uncle Sonny died of liver cancer. I was learning at an earlier age than many of my peers, that death was indeed part of life. But it still stung each time, and these immense questions all revolving around the infinite *why?* loomed in front of me, much like "The Wall" Kerry had described.

After working a year in radio, I was becoming established in a career in the music world, having secured a management position at a leading music retail chain in Chicago. I had a nice apartment, a paid-off car, and a wide circle of friends in and around "the biz." But I knew there was so much more to life... there had to be. Somehow I had to "break on through to the other side." If God was going to help me make sense of all of this, He was going to have to reveal Himself beyond just these books and provocative talks.

To pass beyond is what I seek, I fear that I may be too weak
And those are few who've seen it through to glimpse the other side
The promised land is waiting like a maiden
That is soon to be a bride
The moment is a masterpiece, the weight of indecision's in the air

Gold and diamonds cast a spell, it's not for me I know it well
The riches that I seek are waiting on the other side
There's more than I can measure
In the treasure of the love that I can find
And though it's always been with me,
I must tear down the Wall and let it be
All I am, and all that I was ever meant to be, in harmony

(Kansas, "The Wall," from *Leftoverture,* 1976)

CHAPTER 9

A STRANGE ABERRATION

So as you push off from the shore
Won't you turn your head once more
And make your peace with everyone?
For those who choose to stay
Will live just one more day
To do the things they should have done

And as you cross the wilderness
Spinning in your emptiness
You feel you have to pray
Looking for a sign
That the Universal Mind
Has written you into his Passion Play

Skating away... skating away
Skating away on the thin ice of the New Day
(Jethro Tull, "Skating Away" from *War Child*, 1975)

It had been three years since my high school friends had died and nearly two since I had graduated from Wheaton College. I was trying to settle into a flow where I wasn't going to let the nagging questions pull me down as much. I wanted to move on as best I could. All of my reading and contemplation trying to come to a resolution about whether there was transcendence, had led me to conclude that there were "three main ways" to look at life:

1. We are all basically good, and everyone will enjoy eternal bliss once we shed our mortal coil.
2. We are in a flawed condition and need to justify our way to heaven/God/The Great Cosmic Muffin by earning with copious amounts of meditating, good deeds, holiness, and disciplined living according to a strict code.
3. Everything that has occurred in the universe has been a haphazard culmination of atoms randomly crashing together in various ways, and is, ultimately, quite pointless.

Depending on my mood, I might vacillate between these three or various mutant combinations thereof.

Kerry and I continued to have long discussions in person and on the phone. Just as Kansas was getting ready to record *Monolith,* he called quite excitedly one night telling me of his newest revelation. He had discovered an obscure collection of writings called *The Urantia Book.* He claimed that it was the ultimate answer to every question he had ever had about the cosmos, mankind's development, and spirituality. It was basically a history of the universe as penned by a group of archangels, life carriers, and seraphic hosts. Pretty far out stuff... but what the hey... it sounded fascinating.

It's a strange aberration, this brainstorm of youth
Though it's lost in translation from fancy to truth
It's hopelessly human, both inside and out
A joyous occasion, no reason to doubt
It's easy somehow, what once was elusive is calling me now

(Kansas, "Hopelessly Human" from *Point of Know Return*, 1977)

I initially checked it out of my local library, but due to its 2,097 pages, I couldn't read it all in just a few weeks. So I went ahead and bought it. One of the oddest qualities of *Urantia* was the final quarter of the book entitled: "The Life and Teachings of Jesus," which included a lot of back story on his teenage years, journeys to Greece and Rome, debates with philosophers, etc.

However, because there were no traceable sources for these intriguing but capricious claims, it created skepticism. And I started to compare it with original source materials from the New Testament about Jesus. In reading through the Gospels, I began to register with his story more than I had in the previous several years. He was refreshing in his candor: a much different view than what I had concluded from the "Three Main Ways."

Kerry and I continued to have involved chats about *Urantia*. I especially remember one night at Alpine Valley Music Theater in southern Wisconsin where we spoke for four hours. The nagging question that *Urantia* failed to cover was the need for any sort of redemption for mankind. It seemed that the upshot of all creation was summed up in way #1 listed above. Jesus' demise was explained as a misunderstanding, and despite his inappropriate death, we were to learn from what he taught.

I couldn't help but continue to wrestle with the concept of original sin. It was obvious that we were incapable of consistently following any kind of a steady moral compass on our own. The insanity of our history proved it, and if I needed any further evidence, all I had to do was look in the mirror each morning. Sure I was "more moral" than most others in my profession, but when brutally honest, I knew I was a schmuck.

Desperation shows its ugly face in many ways
No one can escape the times we live in
The answers are so simple and we all know where to look
But it's easier to just avoid the question
(Kansas, "On the Other Side" from *Monolith,* 1979)

Six months passed, and Kansas was coming to Chicago to headline the International Amphitheater on their *Monolith* Tour. Kerry called the day before, setting up the details of our regular visit after the first show. There was an excited urgency in his voice that seemed different than normal. "We *really* need to talk," he pleaded.

The backstage area was crowded with lots of Chicago media, groupies, and various hangers-on. Rick Neilson from Cheap Trick, with whom I was also an acquaintance, was creating his normal boisterous mayhem. Kerry found us a corner and opened up a bag with at least ten books that he placed on a table and nervously stated that he had a lot of new stuff to share. Just then Rick and I made eye contact from about thirty feet away, and he started flicking guitar picks at us as only he can (with his uncanny accuracy). After several of them found my and Kerry's heads, Kerry realized this was not a good locale for sharing heavy spiritual dialogue. He proposed, "You just wanna meet me back at the Hilton where we can have some quiet?"

So, about an hour later when I arrived at his room, he opened the door to reveal all of these texts open in a semi-circle around the foot of his bed. He had obviously been doing a great deal of research on something and wanted to show me his findings in detail. He kind of hemmed and hawed for a while trying to show me, but he was both wound up and sheepish. I'd never seen him this way.

After stumbling through several attempts to show me that *The Urantia Book* was misleading and even false, I said, "Kerry... no worries, man. I found it stimulating to read, but I never believed that it was actually true. It has been helpful, though, in getting me to search back through the Bible at some things that Jesus actually said."

"Oh...that's such a relief!" Kerry exclaimed. But I could tell he was still uneasy as he started fumbling through another one of the books.

"Kerry, I can tell you're on edge," I interjected. "Why don't you put the book down and just tell me what's going on?"

"Well," he paused timidly, closing the book. "I... um... well, I just might as well tell you straight out... I've become a born again Christian."

All my life I knew you were waiting, revelation anticipating
All is well, the search is over, let the truth be known
Let it be shown (give me a glimpse of home)

When I hear your voice
I know I have the choice
To pursue an ideal, something so real
Now I've got nothing to lose

As I see your reflection
All the answers I desire become so clear
Like a page that is turning

I can look into the future without fear

(Kansas, "Glimpse of Home," from *Monolith*, 1979)

It was one of those moments when a truckload of emotions hit me simultaneously. Where I was suddenly overwhelmed by something I simply wasn't expecting. And it left me tied in knots. Because Kerry had flirted about with so many varying spiritual concepts in the past three years I'd known him, let alone in the previous decade of his quest for meaning, I guess I'd never pondered that he might actually consider Christianity. We had certainly talked about it in our long forays into all things spiritual, but we had both dismissed it due to the bevy of frustrations we had with church hypocrites, institutionalized decay, and personal disappointment.

On one hand, I was borderline angry that he was moving in this direction. I was also amazed that he had the balls to share it with me, since I knew how awkward he felt about it. But a third sensation hit me: joy. As I sat there speechless, it was as if a big red neon sign over Kerry's smiling face was flashing, "Answer to prayer! Answer to prayer!" Way back when I started getting into Kansas' music five years earlier, I had made it a point to pray for Kerry specifically more than anyone else in the band. I was just so drawn to his music and his lyrical searching that I knew he wanted God's intervention. And now, for whatever reason, it was like God nudging me... reminding me... even winking at me saying, "See... I'm still here."

Kerry then proceeded to tell me how Jeff Pollard, the lead singer from LeRoux—a band that had opened some dates for Kansas earlier on this tour—had shown him how *The Urantia Book* was full of errors. He also showed Kerry how the Bible was a much more reliable source, and Kerry began to see for the first time that Jesus was truly remarkable in what he claimed... that he wasn't just a good teacher... he was so much more.

After working through a lot for this—over a week of deep discussion and reflection—Kerry made a leap of faith on his own, sitting alone in his hotel room. Never had he been seized by such a power of great affection. Most of his spiritual quest had been head knowledge, but this was a deep inner peace that lifted the burden of all he'd carried for so long. Here it was just two days later, and I was only the second person he had told (the other being his pastor from his youth whom he had called the day before).

While Kerry was chattering away as excitedly as I'd ever seen him, my mixed feelings started to dissipate and my pride started to well up. I wasn't going to be swept into this as well. I had invested much too much pain and harsh interrogation of Christianity for this one little testimony to make a change in what I had endured. Within ten minutes, I started asking him hard questions about Biblical inerrancy, predestination, God's perfect will vs. His permissive will, etc.

I know this was cruel to do to a trusting friend who had just been so vulnerable and whose brand new faith was tender and sweet to him. But I figured if he couldn't take this line of confrontation from me, then he would sure as hell have difficulty with others in the very near future.

Besides, I was fearful of him being abducted by the Christian subculture and suddenly thrust into their little limelight... you know, suddenly becoming a spokesperson for them and all things Jesus. After all, Kansas was one of the five biggest bands in America at that point, and Kerry's music and lyrics was the primary source of that popularity.

But rather than scold me for my cynicism, Kerry calmly shared what he had been reading, and more importantly, experiencing. He was not about to be swayed. It was obvious that he was indeed a different person... a great peace emanated from him.

The discussion went back and forth, hour after hour. At one point we noticed that the sun was coming up, but we kept talking. By 7 AM, we were both toast. He had to prepare to leave for their next gig, and I had to get cleaned up to go into work. We agreed to keep the lines of communication open.

As I drove through Windy City rush hour, my eyes were bleary from the long night, but also from misting over several times. While I was happy for Kerry, I was perplexed... even tormented. Could this really have happened? Now that he felt he had finally "arrived," where would that leave me? One of my best cohorts in "the search" was embarking in a direction I couldn't comprehend. A swirling eddie of debris cut across the Kennedy Expressway, and I was pondering how alone—even pointless—that I felt.

I close my eyes, only for a moment and the moment's gone
All my dreams pass before my eyes a curiosity
Dust in the wind, all they are is dust in the wind

Same old song, just a drop of water in an endless sea
All we do crumbles to the ground though we refuse to see
Dust in the wind, all we are is dust in the wind

(Kansas, "Dust In The Wind" from *Point of Know Return*, 1977)

CHAPTER 10

NOT HUMAN ENOUGH

Touching, we are moving to the things we feel
Trying to be what we could never be
Turning, if we'd only open up our hearts
Yearning, for the things we cannot see
Windows to the world are what we're looking through
Who knows if what we find is true
Seeing is believing as some people say
Knowing is to get a better view

(Kansas, "Windows" from *Vinyl Confessions*, 1982)

Kerry was calling every few days to see how I was doing. He knew that I was vexed. I called a few of my other Christian friends to discuss what had happened with his conversion. They knew that Kerry and I were good friends and that we had been analyzing so many spiritual paths together. They tempered their joy over Kerry's new life with concern over my frustration. They knew too well that I wasn't just gonna waltz back into the faith that easily.

But rather than sinking into bitterness about it, my resolution was strengthened to keep digging. And something wondrous began happening. It seemed like no matter what I read in a newspaper, magazine, or book, or what movie or TV program I saw, or what conversation I had... God, and specifically Christ, seemed to be popping up all the time. I hadn't sensed this kind of interacting where I was being spiritually pursued, in at least four years. It was the proverbial Hound of Heaven chasing after me.

I began to notice that other prayers I had prayed years before had been getting answered: friends with severe health issues, job situations for relatives, resolve in heavy interpersonal issues that others were experiencing. Of course not every intercession I could recall had been addressed... but I was just more receptive to seeing how God was, indeed, at work in areas that I had been distracted from.

I re-read C.S. Lewis' *The Great Divorce* and was drawn toward his view that we may choose to stay in Hell: by our unwillingness to let go of bitterness, superiority, lust, jealousy, and all manner of dysfunctions that have their root in pride. And in many ways, my path had been dictated by a deep vanity that I could somehow figure my fate on my own—and that any flaws in my personality could somehow be rationalized. But it was becoming clearer that the vast majority of my morass was my own doing... my own choice... and I was becoming ever more doubtful of my ability to extricate myself from the consequences.

No one is blameless
But we're all without shame
We fight the fire while we're feeding the flames
Folks have got to make choices
And choices got to have voices
"Folks are basically decent"
Conventional wisdom would say

But we read about the exceptions
In the papers every day

It ought to be second nature
At least, that's what I feel
Now I lay me down in Dreamland
I know perfect's not for real
I thought we might get closer
But I'm ready to make a deal

(Rush, "Second Nature" from *Hold Your Fire*, 1987)

Six weeks later, I awoke early one morning pondering Socrates and how he faced death: not just the heavy questions about the finite nature of our earthly existence, but the literal end when he was forced to drink the hemlock poison for his crime against Athens. Here was one of the more brilliant thinkers of all time: a self-made, self-assured man... greatly respected and full of knowledge... who thought logically and panic-free as he contemplated his ultimate demise.

I juxtaposed this with Christ as he labored heavily with God the Father in the Garden of Gethsemane the night before his arrest, mockery of a trial, severe scourging, and agonizing crucifixion. He expressed his doubt and excruciating anxiety again several times during the next day, but he did so with tremendous resolve. He chose to face that torturous death head-on, for he believed the triumphant good that would come of it. It dawned on me that I could identify with him so much more than Socrates. Christ struck me as truly human at that moment... perhaps the most fulfilled human that ever lived. When I really began looking at Jesus, I started to realize not that I was too human in comparison... but perhaps that

I was not human enough. He exposed a raw depth of reality that no one else ever has.

This is why, I concluded, that Jesus is uniquely qualified to be Savior. He understood that all of the severity of this life had purpose: that sacrifice brings about renewal. It was also becoming clearer to me that if Jesus was allowed to question the Father's will—and even to express doubt and frustration as he hung on that Roman torture tree—then it was OK for me to do the same. I contemplated other personalities from scripture like Job, Abraham, Jacob, Rahaab, Jeremiah, Mary, David, Solomon, Paul, and more who wrestled openly with God... and yet He did not smite them. As a matter of fact, He not only allowed their hard questions but seemed to like that sort of passionate interaction. The Bible was starting to look more like a collection of stories about broken people whom God was trying desperately to encourage and woo back to what He had intended in fellowship with Man.

When Jacob wrestled the angel in Genesis, it was exhausting and tiring. And by the time he finished (and won), his hip was injured. It hurt, and he walked away limping. It dawned on me that when you wrestle with God, it can cause a permanent limp. Some people have no scars—no hobble in their giddy-up—because they haven't tangled with the Omnipotent. The words of G.K. Chesterton resonated deeply: "The Christian ideal has not been tried and found wanting; it has been found difficult and left untried."

I've been boxed-in in the lowlands, in the canyons that think
I've been pushed to the brink of the precipice and dared not to blink
I've been confounded in the whirlwind of what-ifs and dreams
I've been burned by the turning of the wind
Back upon my own flames

I don't want to be lonely, I don't want to feel pain

I don't want to draw straws with the sons of Cain

You can take it as a prayer if you'll remember my name

You can take it as the penance of a profane saint

Knock the scales from my eyes

Knock the words from my lungs

I want to cry out

It's on the tip of my tongue

(Mark Heard, "Tip Of My Tongue" from *Satellite Sky*, 1992)

God wasn't afraid of my questions. In fact, He wanted me to embrace them. It was becoming clearer to me that to truly follow Him, I'd have to regularly see the need for questions. I didn't need to be fearful of my questions; what seemed scary to me was when other people didn't seem to have any or didn't utter them. And a faith that has no room for them is a travesty. Perhaps God was looking for people who won't just blindly accept anything but who want to nakedly ask... to be vulnerable to learn... to be spirited enough to strive, and when all is said and done—when we realize we simply cannot comprehend so much of the never-ending cosmos—that there's a humility that comes from asking wondrous questions of the creator. Like Sean Penn once said: "When everything gets answered, it's fake. The mystery *is* the truth."

Rob Bell offers his take: "The very nature of Christian faith is that we never come to the end. It begs for more. More discussion, more debate, more inquiry, more questions. It's not so much that the Christian faith *has* a lot of paradoxes. It's that it *is* a lot of paradoxes. And we cannot resolve a paradox. Maybe being a Christian is more about celebrating the mystery than conquering it."

Bono admits: "Becoming a Christian didn't give me all the answers. If anything, it gave me a whole new list of questions."

I found myself wanting to echo the sentiment of Rainer Rilke by "living the questions in and through my life."

I was coming to believe that in a paradox, the opposites do not negate each other... they form a mysterious unity. Really, they need each other for balance and context. But in our culture that often demands definitive answers to the conundrums of paradox, we want light without darkness, pleasure without pain: the glories of spring and summer without the demands of fall and winter. Parker J. Palmer sees it like this: "When we so fear the dark that we demand light around the clock, there can be only one result: artificial light that is glaring and graceless and, beyond its borders, a darkness that grows ever more terrifying as we try to hold it off. Split off from each other, neither darkness nor light is fit for human habitation. But if we allow the paradox of darkness and light to be, the two will conspire to bring wholeness and health to every living thing."

There has to be an invisible sun
It gives its heat to everyone
There has to be an invisible sun
It gives us hope when the whole day's done
(Police, "Invisible Sun" from *Ghost In The Machine*, 1981)

Perhaps I had been way too much of a literalist in my earlier days of faith... which had helped lead to my troubles. It's much more esoteric. And I was seeing Jesus' place in all that. He sheds light on everything, while simultaneously allowing for the dark to bring dimension and meaning.

There's a big difference between discovery and revelation. I was trying to unveil lots of information, but what I was really getting was an invitation.

Could it be I was one of those people who reasoned that once I could have all the answers to my doubts and questions, then I would follow God? If so, that would most likely mean I would be waiting a very long time, because ultimately, if I were to know everything, then I would *be* God. Jesus' invitation to jump into an ongoing relationship—even without all the solutions—was exhilarating... even freeing.

And the question about why there couldn't be multiple ways to God wasn't as frustrating to me anymore. I was just glad that God had created *a* way through Jesus. When Jonas Salk found a vaccine for polio, did a bunch of people complain that there wasn't more than one cure? Of course not. We all celebrated that there was now a way to conquer this horrible disease. And the silly tendencies we have to complain became more evident. I mean, if there were sixteen proven ways to come to God, then some of us would ask why there weren't seventeen or eighteen, or 744.

> *I believe in the kingdom come*
> *When all the colors will bleed into one*
> *But yes, I'm still running*
>
> *You broke the bonds and you loosed the chains*
> *Carried the cross of my shame*
> *You know I believe it*
> *But I still haven't found what I'm looking for*
> (U2, "I Still Haven't Found What I'm Looking For" from *The Joshua Tree*, 1987)

CHAPTER 11

STRIPPED BUT NOT AFRAID

I sensed more and more that Jesus was inviting me to join him on this journey, not just for my own sake, but also to help make this world a better place. What he had to offer was so much more appealing than any other shamans, prophets, or philosophers that I had been studying. It seemed that being generous was the best way to live; forgiving others and not swimming in bitterness was the best way to live; having compassion and seeking peace in all situations was the best way to live; gleaning wisdom from others and being honest with myself and those around me was the best way to live. Jesus encapsulated all of these attributes better than anyone else. His view of reality resonated to my core. If I were going to follow someone's lead (and let's be honest, we all follow someone), he seemed to come in head and shoulders above the rest.

Another couple of weeks passed in which I spoke openly of my contemplation of returning to my faith in Christ. I even had meetings with good friends like Rick, Scott, Tammy, and Ron, who weren't believers. They knew me pretty well and encouraged me, saying that it made sense to them that I refocus my life in this way. Ron said, "It doesn't seem like a matter of *if* you return, but a matter of *when.*"

The regular phone chats with Kerry continued, as did discussions with other believers who had stuck with me through the dark times. I also had some long talks with my Dad about heavy theological issues. Even with his seminary degrees, he reassured me that trying to put the microscope to God was simply not going to work.

"We want to build all this scaffolding around God, feeling that we might somehow contain him and try to analyze minutia. But a god like that is way too small. He simply will not be restricted by our imaginings. He is raw and untamed but ultimately very, very good to us," Dad said.

I knew that if I were to ever move forward, I was going to have to set my pride aside. I was going to have to admit I was incapable of sorting out my own dilemma, let alone the machinations of the universe. I needed to surrender.

Now I am stripped
I am naked
I am humbled but not betrayed
And your love beyond expression
Laid bare my heart's remains
I am stripped
But not afraid

(Rick Elias, "Stripped" from *Rick Elias And The Confessions*, 1990)

In the midst of another sleepless night, on Sept. 12th, 1979 at 2:30 AM, I opened the empty hands of faith. There was no altar call. There was no gnashing of teeth and wallowing in remorse. And there were certainly no emotional fireworks. I simply made a vow to trust Him. No matter what.

I murmured under my breath, "Circumstances don't mean shit. I am going to do this, and I will not be swayed by overly negative events or hypocrites—including me. I don't even want good things happening to influence me. This is all about what you, Jesus, are going to do in molding me into your image. It could very well be hard much of the time, but I want the peace that you promise."

I lay very still in bed for another half hour, not sensing much of anything except a bit of relief. The next morning I awoke with a raging headache. For some reason the hot water heater had gone out, and my shower was icy. While driving to work, I had a flat tire. Then it began to rain while changing it. When I finally arrived at my record store, my assistant manager called in sick, and I had to tend to twice my normal duties. But through all of that I recalled my vow: "These things are not of consequence. I have done the right thing. I will not be deterred."

And if the darkness is to keep us apart
And if the daylight feels like it's a long way off
And if your glass heart should crack
And for a second you turn back
Oh no, be strong
You're packing a suitcase for a place none of us has been
A place that has to be believed to be seen
You could have flown away
A singing bird in an open cage
Who will only fly for freedom

Walk on, walk on
What you got they can't steal it
No they can't even feel it
Walk on, walk on
(U2, "Walk On" from *All That You Can't Leave Behind*, 2001)

During the following week, I began letting different friends know of my decision, including Kerry. There were no dramatic histrionics... but there was a tender welcome back and an assurance that they would continue to stick with me no matter what.

A search for a fellowship where I would be allowed to work through my hard questions led me to Winnetka Bible Church. They had a singles group there that had thoughtful Bible studies, and I helped form a support group that allowed us to be gut-level honest in our ongoing quest as well as consoled and energized in our communal bond.

Coming back as I did, I knew that things would be different in my faith this time through. My candidness was sometimes off-putting to the ecumenical crowd. And my commitment to following Christ was sometimes an irritant to the many I interacted with daily in the music biz. Mark Heard summed it up when he sang, "I'm too sacred for the sinners, and the saints wish I would leave." And sometimes I would wince when I'd think back on how I'd been raised and ill prepared for the pain I experienced.

When I was young and they packed me off to school
And taught me how not to play the game
I didn't mind if they groomed me for success
Or if they said that I was a fool

So I left there in the morning
With their God tucked underneath my arm
Their half-assed smiles and the book of rules
So I asked God a question
And by way of firm reply He said
"I'm not the kind you have to wind up on Sundays"

So to my old headmaster and to anyone who cares

Before I'm through I'd like to say my prayers

I don't believe you

You had the whole damn thing all wrong

He's not the kind you have to wind up on Sundays

(Jethro Tull, "Wind Up" from *Aqualung,* 1972)

I really began to focus on Jesus' teaching. Those red letters carry a tremendous amount of weight... They cleansed me and kept things simple, but very profound. And overall, I was filling with his peace. I owned up to my mistakes, asked his forgiveness and began to rest in the wisdom of accepted tenderness he had toward me. And likewise, finding other honest seekers and thinkers like Kerry has been invaluable in my journey.

As for all the hard questions... many of them still remained. My heart still ached for Ernie, John, Mike, and others who had died while struggling in their faith journey. Doubts still lingered regarding certain elements of scripture and the nature of God as portrayed in the Old Testament. I found that dwelling on them rarely solves anything. Much smarter and more spiritual predecessors than I had been crushed under their weight. That didn't mean I wasn't still trying to carry them from time to time. And I certainly hurled them at God on occasion when the absurdity of it all got overwhelming.

But then I would remember that *peace* is mentioned 360 times in the Bible; God wanted me to enter into his rest. Over and over in the scriptures, whenever he presented himself to someone, the first words were: "Do not fear." I chose to live in that assurance as best I could rather than fighting or fleeing.

The Creator was infinitely wise in designing seasons as the primary movement of life. Parker Palmer wrote that it's not a battlefield or a game of chance, but something infinitely richer, more promising, more real. The notion that our lives are like the eternal cycle of the seasons does not deny the struggle or the joy, the loss or the gain, the darkness or the light, but encourages us to embrace it all—and to find in all of it opportunities for growth.

> *These are the seasons of emotion*
> *And like the winds they rise and fall*
> *This is the wonder of devotion*
> *I see the torch we all must hold*
> *This is the mystery of the quotient:*
> *Upon us all a little rain must fall*
>
> (Led Zeppelin, "The Rain Song" from *Houses of the Holy*, 1973)

CHAPTER 12

TAMING A MOUNTAIN RAM

As the '70s came to a close, my brother, Jim, became involved with a nice girl named Brenda. They lived together for a while, and she began to realize that if they were ever going to get serious, she would have to make the move. She actually proposed to *him*, pointedly asking him if he would marry her. He shrugged his shoulders and said, "Yeah, I guess so." So they got one of those Nevada licenses during a quickie trip to Las Vegas.

They ended up moving to Denver where he had learned there was a growing music scene. We started hearing from them quite often, as Brenda loved the idea of family and sent us all birthday and Christmas cards (although she usually signed for him) as well as calling us much more regularly than Jim would ever do on his own.

Once while having dinner with my folks, when Joyce was in her junior year in college, we had a long heart-to-heart about Jim. Dad confessed that perhaps he had been an absentee father during Jim's formative years, being involved with struggling congregations that needed so much of his time. I proffered my theory that so many first-borns are really an experiment—guinea pig of sorts—for young parents. They learn a lot from their mistakes, and hopefully the next several aren't as problematic. We talked about so many other families we knew that had gone through similar challenges with their initial child, especially in the turbulent '60s. Mom teared up several times feeling so forlorn about Jim's anger, resentment, and rebellion.

As the new decade began, my parents had moved to serve an inner city church in Philadelphia, and Joyce graduated from Wheaton. Jim continued to scuffle along with various band gigs in the Rocky Mountains, occasionally getting a sniff from an A&R director, but more often than not, toiling away in anonymity. He started sending me demo tapes to get my opinions... which meant a lot. I think he realized he was probably never going to "make it," but that he was good enough to play in several of the top cover bands along the Front Range and was making an OK living from it.

By 1982, I had relocated to Nashville and had become the manager for Petra, whom I had known for 10 years at that point. I'll never forget when I got a rather hysterical call from my mother on a chilly October morning saying, "Your father has been having some pretty serious issues with concentration and short term memory loss lately. He's had some tests done..." She paused. There was a definite catch in her voice "...And the doctor here thinks he might only have... six months to two years to live."

You see, Alzheimer's had just recently been "discovered" by the medical community, and it became the diagnosis de jour for anyone with retention issues at that time. Of course my Mom was frantic, but Dad wanted to get further tests and opinions before relenting to that prognosis.

After I got her calmed down on the phone, she hesitated and then asked, "Do you think I should call Jim and let him know?"

How strange that our Mother felt so meek about letting her eldest son know about a life-threatening situation to his father. But this was the nature of how Jim had come to control our family: we walked on eggshells around him, because we didn't want to feel his sarcasm or the pain that he brought from his indifference. He had hurt my folks in particular so many times before.

Even though we both agreed that he might mock—possibly even derisively laugh—I said that she needed to be strong and tell him. "I really think he would appreciate knowing, Mom."

Later that afternoon out in Colorado, Brenda came in from work to find Jim pacing back and forth nervously in the living room clouded with cigarette fumes. She had never seen him so distressed and knew something was surely wrong, because he had given up smoking the year before.

"What's wrong, honey?" she offered. He just kept frantically walking about and couldn't seem to gather his thoughts. "Please, Jim, what is it?"

He stopped, looked at her with an anguish she had never experienced, and all the color drained from his face. "My Dad is dying!" he blurted out, and began to sob.

Since we had no idea if the medical assessment was solid or not, we all decided to get together for Thanksgiving in Philly. Isn't it sad that it is often tragic events that start to bring families back together? All three of us children and Brenda determined in advance calls with each other that we were going to keep things upbeat—but honest—in our time together. After all, who knew how long Dad might be with us?

I think we began to mend that holiday. We played board games together for the first time since the mid '60s. We reminisced fondly about neighborhood antics in Columbus growing up. We even joked about some of the strange clothes and alliances Jim had gotten into, and all admitted to various other foibles of our own. We laughed. We shed a few tears. We hugged. Some of my favorite photos of our family were captured that week. No apologies on either side were tendered... but it was a good start.

Through my connections with the music world, I was able to get Jim, Brenda, and myself some decent seats to see Genesis at the Philadelphia Spectrum. He was impressed that I knew how to get things like that done in such short order and amazed that I actually knew my way around backstage, conversing with crew, road managers, and so on.

As months moved forward, my parents did get several other results from tests, showing that what Dad was suffering from was indeed *not* fatal. With improved dietary adjustments, better sleep patterns, and certain medications, he would most likely recover... and he did. Makes my blood boil now thinking how reckless many physicians can be with inaccurate assessments that throw everyone into chaos. Of course, we were overjoyed, especially when the new procedures bore positive fruit. Perhaps God used that poor diagnosis to bring Jim back toward us.

Moving through the mid-80s, communication continued to increase between Jim and the rest of the Hollingsworth clan. Brenda was a big part of that, for sure... but Jim genuinely seemed more interested. I had always given him samples of Christian rock I was involved with, and he seemed particularly interested in what I was doing with Petra as their manager. They were selling millions of albums, getting airplay on MTV, and selling out shows all across North America, Europe, and Australia.

Whenever they would tour through Denver, I would fly out to see him and allow he and as many of his friends as possible into the shows and to wander around backstage. The band was always very kind toward him, making him and his buddies feel right at home. Jim had become a pretty decent photographer, and he'd be clicking away on his deluxe Canon 35mm camera with all sorts of lenses before, during, and after the big productions we staged. "Who would've thought my little brother could ever do anything like this?" he joked to his friends during a backstage meal one night at the sold out Red Rocks Amphitheater.

Upon visiting his home in the summer of '84, I was pleasantly surprised to find that he had enlarged and mounted some stellar concert shots he had taken of the band. He'd also framed several of their album covers as well as concert posters they had signed for him, and he had them proudly displayed in his living room and den.

Two years later, due to the stresses of the band's explosive growth, I decided to leave Petra. I was offered a job with Compassion International, whom I had been pursuing for possible employment on and off for six years. I don't think it was any coincidence that they had relocated to Colorado Springs, just sixty miles south of where Jim and Brenda lived. It was thrilling to work for such a great ministry helping poor children and being so much closer to my brother.

For the first time since we were little dudes, Jim and I were hanging out again and really enjoying each other's company. Whether it was going to hear him play at some of the best clubs in Denver, attending cookouts he threw with his buddies, going to concerts (three of the best were Bob Seger, Don Henley, and John Mellencamp—all mutual faves of ours), hiking, going to movies, or just playing fetch with his crazed dingo, Smokey, we were having a blast. We weren't just becoming brothers again... we were becoming great friends.

One evening while we were watching a baseball game, he told me he had not only quit using needles five years before, but that he'd also quit smoking dope. He was feeling so much better, although it was still nearly impossible for him to put any meat on his six-foot-two-inch 165 pound frame. He always joked about his "bird cage physique."

After being there for eighteen months, Jim felt like it would be cool to invite the whole family out for vacation in May of '87. Joyce, Mom, Dad, Jim, Brenda, and I convened at their home for Memorial Day week. We went hiking in Big Bear National Park, went sightseeing in Denver's historic district, tooled around Estes Park up in the Rockies, had some cookouts, and had lots of relaxed fun just chatting. We were all a bit stunned when Jim offered to lead the prayer over a couple of meals. I had also noticed for the first time that he had a Bible on the end table next to his favorite lazy boy recliner that had some passages underlined.

Even though there were not any direct discussions about faith, let alone forgiveness, it sure seemed that Jim was in transition of sorts. We all knew better than to overtly push the subject—it had precipitated so much argument and ill-will in the past that it just wasn't worth trying to "define" what he was evolving toward. We just wanted to encourage him to find his own way back toward the flock, because we knew this particular black sheep was not about to be shepherded very easily.

Less than a month later something would happen that would change everything forever...

CHAPTER 13

SHORN

I have a love/hate relationship with Christian music festivals. I've been to over ninety of them either as a manager or working with Compassion's artist relations department. I've dealt with mud up to my mid-calf, breathing dust and charcoal-filled air for days on end, 100+ degree swelter fests, bad (and usually overly loud) sound systems, inedible carnival food, and more than my share of feculent bands glorifying the Lord with god-awful music. And I've seen every sad mutation of pop culture colloquialisms twisted even further in the form of "Jesus Wear" T-shirts. You know... *This Blood's For You, Air Jesus* (instead of *Air Jordan*), *Book of Daniel* (with logo like Jack Daniel's Whiskey), and crappola like that.

But my heart has also been warmed by some amazing performances from truly gifted musicians like the aforementioned Keaggy, Livgren's AD, Steve Taylor, The Swirling Eddies, Mark Heard, Jars of Clay, and Ashley Cleveland. And profound communicators like Tony Campolo, Brennan Manning, John Perkins, Wess Stafford, and Mike Yaconelli have given me a fresh glimpse into a relevant faith walk in the midst of goofy poop like Carmen, Stryper, DC Talk, Mike Warnke, and Pat Robertson.

The grand daddy of 'em all is Creation Fest in central Pennsylvania, which has been held annually since the late '70s. It might not be the oldest (Ichthus in Kentucky holds that distinction from 1970 onward), but Creation is by far the biggest and best run. I think I've been to it eleven times, along with at least 60,000 other confused souls who think congregating in the steamy, rounded mountains near Altoona in late June is a good idea.

It was with this backdrop that one of the landmark days of my life occurred. June 27th, 1987: it was the second day of the four-day fest. My buddy Dan Hickling had been hired to assist me in running our Compassion booth, where we hoped to get at least 500 needy kids sponsored. At around ten-o-clock that morning, one of the festival staff summoned me to the lone phone in our shed of around forty exhibitors. Some lousy Christian metal band was grinding away on the main stage 300 yards away at the base of the hill below us, and the thumping volume was literally making sawdust sprinkle down from the rafters of the old wooden structure on every thunderous downbeat.

Holding any normal conversation in that environment was hard enough, and upon picking up the phone, I quickly realized it would be nearly impossible to tell who was on the other end of the line, let alone what they were trying to tell me. On top of that, there was a short in the cord, and I was only hearing about two-thirds of what the caller was saying. It was someone from the festival's main office (which was right next to stage area) relaying a message. Through this crackling maze, I heard someone asking me if Jim Hollingsworth was my brother... that he had been rushed to St. Joseph Hospital in Denver... that I needed to call the emergency room there for more info. I couldn't really understand what they were saying, so I hung up and dialed zero. After about twenty rings, someone finally answered and we were practically yelling at each other trying to be heard over the blessed chaos spewing from the stage.

They were kind enough to patch me through to an outside operator. Through fits and starts of fragmented conversation, she was able to connect me to that hospital. Upon reaching the main switchboard, a wild goose chase began trying to figure out if my brother was there. Though garbled because of the excruciating bluster of band noise, I spoke with several folks in various departments, none of whom knew of a James David Hollingsworth who had been admitted there. I was quite befuddled until one of them said, "Oh... maybe he's at the *other* St. Joseph Hospital." What dunderhead came up with the idea of having two hospitals in the same city with identical names? Geesh.

So, the guy then gives me the phone number, which I remember scrawling onto a used hotdog wrapper I picked up off the gritty floor. I redialed the festival operator, asking if I could come down and use their phone there. She laughed out loud, saying, "If you think it's hard to hear up there, imagine what it's like down here!" But she was kind enough to finally get to another outside operator who would then let me charge a call to my credit card. I thanked God, both literally and facetiously, due to the band stopping their inane racket for a moment of testifying between "songs." You can imagine my frustration as I was trying to deal with all of this, while under the surface I was drowning in worry about what had happened to Jim.

I decided to try to call Jim's home number, but I just got his answering machine. I tried my parents, but their line was busy. Same with my sister's.

I finally got through to the *other* St. Joseph and was just beginning to make some headway on being transferred to the emergency room, when the interminable crowing erupted from the stage again—this time even more cacophonous than ever. I heard smatterings of things that sounded like "paramedics," "unconscious," and "cardiac arrest," but I was foiled each time I tried to converse by the musical mayhem surrounding me and the faulty wiring of the phone. The person on the other end was having just as much trouble understanding me. I said I would try to call back in a few minutes from a quieter locale.

Rushing back over to Dan at the booth, I told him something terrible had happened with my brother, and I was going to try to find a better line. "Do whatever you need to," he urged. "I'll hold the fort."

I grabbed the keys to our rental van and proceeded to bob and weave through the festival traffic at about four miles-per-hour (there are rarely roads utilized for just vehicles at these events— just wave after wave of sweaty, disoriented, heat-stroked teens-on-foot clogging the arteries). After about fifteen minutes, I was able to lurch through the soiled throng and get to a service road I knew of that had a "secret" exit out of the grounds. At that point, I gassed that Dodge Econoliner through the narrow backwoods of those Allegheny valleys.

My aim was to stop at one of the many small farmhouses and ask if I could please use their phone to make an emergency call with my AT&T card. No one answered the door at the first. I raced to the next one, and they refused to let me in. At the third, they told me I should just use a pay phone in town. It's at times like these that you really question the compassion of one's fellow man.

Burning rubber out of their driveway, I took that advice and must've been doing close to three digits on the speedometer over those rollercoaster hills (bottoming out several times as I crashed down after going airborne on some crests), racing into Mount Union—a little burg about ten miles from the festival.

Careening through the cramped streets, I spotted a Sheetz convenience store with a pay phone. I fumbled around with my phone card and the scribbled number on the soiled paper... and I finally got through to the hospital and asked if they could tell me about a patient named Jim Hollingsworth who had been admitted to the emergency room an hour or so earlier. I was put on hold several times. I was asked more than a few questions about my own identity.

Finally, after about five minutes of delays, a kind gentleman got on the line. "So you are Jim Hollingsworth's brother?"

"Yes," I huffed for about the fifth time without trying to sound too exasperated.

"I'm so sorry to tell you... but he passed away about an hour ago. He apparently had a massive coronary in his home and was pronounced dead on arrival here."

It was one of those instants that will be etched forever in my mind. A huge lumber truck was passing by, and as it accelerated, a gust of diesel fumes blew in my face. There was a chunky little boy slurping away on a cherry snow cone next to the entrance of the Sheetz. A big Irish setter was barking in the back of a pick-up about fifteen feet away. Life was going on as usual all around me... but death had invaded my existence yet again.

The images of Ernie, Mike, and John, came front and center immediately. That heavy toll bore down within seconds. Here it was a decade later, and all those same feelings began sweeping over me like a tsunami.

"Sir... Mr. Hollingsworth... Mark... are you still there?" asked the gentleman from the Saint Joe's. I don't know how long I had paused... it was only just a few seconds I'm sure, but it felt much, much longer.

"Ahhhh... yes. Yes, I'm here." I stammered. He began giving me some other numbers to call, but I was on autopilot as I was jotting information down. All I could think was, "Well, this is Life. This is how it works: you try to enjoy the good times in between the bottomed-out moments like these. Jim was working his way back... and now... he's gone. Just like those other guys. Yep... this is God-Forsaken Life."

We had been making tremendous strides coming back together as a family... and he'd seemed to be truly coming around after decades of turmoil that had been brewing within himself and had spilled out and been inflicted on the rest of us.

After that moment, the next few days were a blur. Lots of dialing to make arrangements with family, flights, funeral parlors, cemeteries, Compassion staff, festival officials, etc. etc. It's funny how you can take care of myriad details while your heart is torn asunder... shock and grief are odd that way.

I remember lying on the bed in room 127 at the Huntingdon, Pennsylvania Days Inn later that day... staring up at the ceiling with tears running down my cheeks and declaring to God and anyone else who might've been listening: "I am not going to give up my faith again over this... please... God, help me *not* give up on You again. I know You love Jim. I know You love Mom, Dad, Joyce, and me. I don't get it *at all* as to *why* You work like You do. But... please... help me not to lose my faith again."

CHAPTER 14

IN A HIGHLANDS MEADOW

We decided to have a viewing and memorial service for my brother in Denver and then the final funeral and burial in Mt. Vernon, Illinois, which was Brenda's hometown.

Something strange happened over and over again as I conversed with some of Jim's Colorado friends at the funeral home. They told me how much Jim liked Petra and even some of the other artists' albums I had given him, like Russ Taff, Kerry Livgren, The Call, and Phil Keaggy. It wasn't just that he liked the music. He would pull out the liner notes and tell them, "Look at these cool lyrics."

Jim was loved and respected by the music community along the Front Range, and that was evidenced by the amount that came to pay their respects. One of his buddies told me that some of them had been kicking around the idea of forming a new blues band that would, oddly enough, be called The Black Sheep.

In public, we were holding up pretty well... but behind the scenes, it was particularly hard on Mom and Dad. You always hear that there is no greater pain than a parent having to bury their child. And Brenda was much too young to be a widow; she was especially distraught. Joyce and I decided to divert some of our tension by going to see *Spaceballs*. We chortled through the silliness of it all, knowing that Jim would've enjoyed another dose of Mel Brooks' offbeat humor.

In the midst of all this, the irony was not lost on us that our family had experienced such a lovely week together less than a month before. Despite our stinging trial, we were extremely grateful for having that reunion of sorts. Our flock had finally begun feeling whole again after years of disruption from that one dark-wooled wanderer.

After the funeral, my good friend and boss Devlin Donaldson told me that Compassion didn't expect me to cover the remaining festivals if I wasn't up to it. "Take as much time as you need," he implored. Having lost his dad to cancer, Dev was a sensitive soul to the strange inner workings of mourning.

But I felt that "getting back on the horse" might be best for me. I had helped organize the Compassion All-Star Band to play at the Cornerstone festival that began the day after the funeral, and since it was in the same state, I decided to go ahead and help out behind the scenes. The cadre of great musicians who had volunteered to play, and were long-time friends, were all so gracious toward me. Glenn Kaiser, Phil Madeira, and Rick Cua, had very kind and sensitive words. When Randy Stonehill saw me come into the rehearsal room for the first time, he simply came over and without a single word just hugged me for a long time.

After one of the practices, Phil Keaggy said, "Let's get out of here." We drove around for a bit until he spotted a little Irish Pub. It was early afternoon, so he figured it would be quiet. I don't like alcohol much, but Phil went ahead and ordered Guinness Stout for himself. He asked about Jim and let me open up. After a while, he began to share more from his deep well of experience than I had ever heard... about brothers and sisters who had passed away unexpectedly, his mom's death that was so impactful on him as a teen-ager, and about the five children he and Bernadette had lost during childbirth before finally having three healthy kids.

"I don't know about a lot of high-minded theology on the after-life, although I've certainly studied my share," he reasoned. "But I think we're going to be surprised at who is going to be in heaven. And what an encouragement to know that Jesus said all of heaven rejoices when the shepherd finds that one lost lamb—the one that everyone else may have given up on—in the thicket."

A few weeks later I was with Brennan Manning at another fes-tival. Even though our friendship was just in its early stages, he was so incredibly gracious in drawing me out and listening to my con-fession of hurt and doubt. Brennan has also lived through torrents of pain and loss. He said, "I simply don't believe God is vengeful to-ward those who are seeking Him... even if they have been rebel-lious. I think His net of salvation is much bigger and stronger than we would allow with our narrow judgments of others. He knows our hearts so much better than even we do. Even though King David was a scheming, adulterous murderer, God loved him wildly and de-clared that David 'was a man after God's own heart.'"

I admitted to him that I was having trouble praying. He gently put his hand on my shoulder and said, "Since you don't have the strength nor the inclination for now, will you allow me the privilege of praying for you? Let me bring your pain before the Father for a while. When you're ready to start praying again, just let me know."

Over the next month while I was still journeying to festivals, we got word back on Jim's autopsy. His death was so sudden and unex-pected, we all wanted to have a better idea of what happened.

It turns out that he had a very rare congenital disorder known as Marfans Syndrome. We had never heard of it before but did a great deal of research on it in the following weeks. It only turns up every other generation in certain families and affects about one in 50,000. Some of the characteristics of Marfans are being tall and incredibly thin, with long fingers, toes, overly big ears and a long nose—all which fit Jim to a T. It explained why he was so gangly, even as a toddler... no Rickets after all. Famous people who most likely have/have had Marfans include: Abraham Lincoln, Phil Jackson, Kevin McHale, and Ric Ocasek (the leader of the pop band The Cars).

When someone has this rare disease, there's a possibility that their heart, and especially the aorta, can become weakened over time. This is one of the strongest muscles in the body, responsible for pumping blood throughout the entire soft machine. Normally it is as reliable as several coils of extremely strong rubber. However, with Marfans, it can actually deteriorate to more like three layers of wet paper plates... and under the right circumstance, it can tear apart and cause massive internal bleeding.

At seven a.m. that morning of June twenty-seventh; right after the alarm awoke them, Jim and Brenda were lying in bed mulling over who would let the dog out and start brewing that morning's pot of coffee. As she sat on the edge of the bed, Jim suddenly began choking and heaving about, making gurgling sounds. Within ten seconds, the thrashing stopped. It happened that fast. He was gone.

The autopsy report also stated that a decade's worth of substance abuse had not helped anything, either. His insides were a mess, horribly compromised and ravaged by chemicals never intended to be coursing through one's system.

In between my festival trips, I was able to go in for a complete physical and various tests to see if I might have Marfans as well. I was given a clean bill of health.

I was still in the fog of grief while at the Jesus Northwest Festival in Oregon later in July. Tony Campolo pulled me aside, saying,

"Peggy and I heard about your brother and we are so sorry for you and your parents." Tony knew my folks fairly well due to partnering in some inner city missions in Philadelphia.

We chatted a bit in a quiet field out behind the grounds one afternoon. "You know, Mark, on Judgment Day there are going to be a lot of people who are actually stunned that they are going to be invited into heaven, and conversely, there will be many who are so cocksure that they are headed toward their 'eternal reward,' and they are going to be shocked when God tells them, 'Depart from me, for I never knew you.' Matthew twenty-five is clear about that. I'm not saying one way or the other what happened with Jim... but it sure seems like God was drawing him closer. And remember, in Proverbs, we're encouraged to 'raise up a child in the ways of the Lord, and he won't depart from it.' Your brother certainly took some stupid detours, but maybe he was headed back onto the right route. Let that be your and your family's hope."

By the time mid-August rolled around, festival season was complete. A lot of the carnival-like, frivolous atmosphere of each setting had probably not been the best for my soul as I was working through my grief. But, I *had* gotten some good solace in the midst of those traveling circuses from trusted friends along the way, and I'll be grateful for that for the rest of my life.

However, as is often the case in mourning, I was being tense, rude, and biting with those I was with the most: my co-workers in the Compassion office. My superiors pulled me in and told me I *needed* to take some vacation. "Just get away from everything and allow yourself to grieve," was their directive.

So I took a week and journeyed up into the Rockies. No particular agenda each day... in fact, I can't recall much of where I went. I just know I took plenty of long hikes into obscure valleys.

Reflecting back on my relationship with Jim, it suddenly all fell into place for me why I had been drawn into using my organizational skills and passion to promote Christian rock: I was trying to reach Jim. Booking and promoting over a thousand concerts attended by millions of people, all the chart topping singles, helping bands reach gold and platinum status in record sales... it was ultimately all to prove to Jim that Jesus cared for a wayward rocker like him. It was the only thing I felt that would be relevant in helping him understand God's forgiveness and love. For the longest time, he had mocked me and the music... but apparently, it had finally started making an impact in those final few years. But why had his grasping of this been aborted so suddenly? Why was God so cruel?

After several days of quietly assessing it all and mulling it over, I finally felt like talking with God. So, for the first time in months, I really began to pour it out. Sometimes in a conversational tone, sometimes whispering as I traversed the wilderness. Occasionally yelling at the top of my lungs at both Jim and God. I didn't hear anything in return except my own echo bouncing back across rocky crevasses of those canyons. But as I traversed the ragged granite outcroppings and sat among the heather with the wind encircling me, I sensed He was there... just like my loyal friends... allowing me to vent, to purge, and to pray in moanings too deep even for words.

I was really beginning to miss Jim. In the past year, we'd begun to develop a closer bond than we had even had as little guys growing up. We'd been making up for lost time—twenty years of his recklessness. And all the things I had thrown myself into—regarding music and culture to try and somehow reach out to him—seemed pointless to me at that moment. "What's the use now? He's disappeared to who-knows-where."

Seven days of this went by... each with cycles of anger, questions, silence, and some degree of acceptance. I was hurt and lonely. And God was pretty much silent.

Late in that final afternoon of my week off, with sullen clouds gathering for another daily storm, I sat up suddenly after lying for several hours staring and mumbling into the void. I had been startled hearing a cowbell a few hundred feet away. I looked down from my summit at a high mountain meadow to see a flock of sheep that had quietly moved into my realm. Glancing in every direction, there was no other human to be seen. Their shepherd must've trusted them to be on their own for most of each day.

The herd started to move eastward, when what appeared to be the eldest—the one wearing the cowbell—stopped and began to bleat. Others joined in, kind of surveying the topography around them... calling out for something... someone. After a few moments, about thirty yards away, I noticed some rustling in a clump of shrubs, and out bounded a lamb... a black lamb. It sort of shook itself awake and then started its gangly gait towards the others. As they saw the little guy bumbling toward them, they recommenced their trek. Just as he reached them, the whole group disappeared behind a cleft.

I sat motionless.

After not breathing for what seemed like a few minutes, I heaved an immense sigh that came from deep, deep within me... stood up, and started my trip home.

PART TWO

SHADOWS
AND LIGHT

CHAPTER 15

STUCKEY'S WARM FUZZIES

Most of us have heeded the siren call of Stuckey's interstate eateries over the past few generations. On long family vacations, it was a wonderful respite from cramped station wagons full of baggage, stinky feet, and Dad's insistence on listening to nothing but whiny country music or news broadcasts on the tinny AM dashboard radio. No individualized iPods or DVD's in those days.

So when we saw signs for a Stuckey's at the next exit, we knew we were in for a treat. Perhaps a milkshake, or a pecan roll, or some sugar sticks, or a chilled lemonade. They always had much cleaner restrooms than the roadside rest stops or filling stations. Hence; all the way around, they served as an oasis on those elongated treks to places like Cherry Hill, North Carolina; Cripple Creek, Colorado; the World's Fair in Montreal; or St. Louis to see the Arch.

So, once I was on my own as an adult, I still enjoyed the respite of a Stuckey's break on any of my own journeys. One particular time, I had been visiting Phil and Elinor Madeira while they were still in Providence, Rhode Island. Working my way back to Chicago, I decided I would scoot over to Ann Arbor, Michigan in one day's drive. Your mind doesn't perceive that as being that far, but it was perhaps one of the longest solo drives of my life: fourteen hours through sub-zero, icy conditions.

Like my Pop, I'm all about making good time when by myself and rarely stop for long on a trip like that. Fuel up, take a tinkle, hit a drive-thru, and skedaddle. But as I was cruising along I-80 in Pennsylvania, through the beautiful Moshannon State Forest near Penn State University, I saw the familiar script lettering and robin egg blue roof of a Stuckey's in the distance beckoning me. I needed some gas anyway, and stretching my legs and grabbing a tasty snack would help me for the last seven hours that lay ahead.

As I perused the various "home-made" sweets, I laid eyes on some rich brownies with double fudge icing on them, individually wrapped in cellophane and quaint little yellow boxes that looked like Whitman samplers. I bought four of 'em and a Dr. Pepper after topping off my tank, and I sped down the ramp westward into the sunset.

Like most sophisticated Americans, I have learned to do many chores while driving. Talking on the phone, consulting maps, playing air guitar, air drums, and air keyboards... writing notes, reading the paper, and of course, eating. Piloting a 2,500-pound hunk of metal, filled with twenty gallons of highly flammable fluid—at sixty-five miles an hour down sporadically iced stretches of pothole filled northeastern freeway while trying to multi-task—is something one ought to reconsider.

The scene: I open up one of my brownie boxes and wolf it down in just three bites with the caffeinated chaser of D.P. The sugar rush is tangible. Foghat's "Fool For the City" is nearly ripping the speakers out of their sockets in the doors and back mantle. *I've got another 350 miles to go, and nothin's slowing me down!* I'm hummin' along in more ways than one—passing traffic to my right like its almost parked.

The sunset is right on the horizon, causing me to scrunch up my eyes: trying to get the right angle so it doesn't completely blind me. I fumble with brownie number two, discarding the outer cardboard covering, and rip the vacuum-sealed cellophane open with my teeth. I take a bite while holding it in my left hand, my right hand on the wheel. Something seems a bit... *different.* Sort of wet and tangy... but not the same consistency of chocolatey goodness from the first one. Was it a different type of icing? Had I accidentally picked up a berry or carrot cake brownie in my hurried rest stop? I casually turn my wrist to examine what might be the difference...

(Have you ever had an instant when something freaks you out so quickly that for an undetermined spell, you completely lose track of time and your sensory perception of everything around you? This was one of those for me.)

Through eyes that are wincing from the intense orange sun, I see a furry, two-inch slug churning along some primordial slime of its own making on the flip side of said brownie.

I'm a big boy, and insects, snakes, and mice don't normally disturb me. This, however, sends me into absolute bonsai frenzy. Without forethought about what my primary duty is at that moment (namely, driving an eight-cylinder Oldsmobile at seventy-five-plus miles-per-hour), I literally jump out of my seat, ramming my head into the ceiling. In the process, I drop the cake and it's passenger between my legs. I begin spitting brown goo all over the windshield of my car. While trying to keep my hips aloft, I'm madly sweeping my pants and the seat below me, trying to scrape the offender away from my crotch. I'm screaming words that start with "f" and end with "u-c-k," and I don't believe any of them were "firetruck."

Mind you, this is all happening as I'm barreling down a long hill on the interstate, and I just happen to be passing an eighteen-wheeler. As I'm spastically trying to eradicate the slug, my right foot

is pressed much harder on the accelerator, and I'm probably doing ninety-plus and weaving around like an utter imbecile. I come
within inches of swiping the big rig on my right—and just miss the
snowdrifts on my left and the ensuing thick pines. The trucker is
wildly blowing his horn and flashing his lights. I'm sure he thinks
I'm having an epileptic fit... or perhaps having a seizure over something Rush Limbaugh just said.

But that's not the end of it. My adrenaline is pumping like a
bullfighter on Cinco de Mayo. I find remnants of the brownie, but
I CANNOT locate the renegade guest. I'm furious about what has
happened, so I roll down my window and chuck out what's left of
my "tasty repast," along with the third brownie, the fourth brownie,
all the empty wrappers, the bag, the napkins, even the Dr. Pepper—
each item one at a time—accompanied with another swerving motion from my careening Cutlass and more vitriolic adverbs. This
erratic behavior causes the trucker, who has now slowed to a pace
several hundred feet behind me, to continue blasting and flashing.

Being embarrassed and angry, I put the pedal to the proverbial
metal and must be doing over a hundred as I rocket ahead into the
sunset. I stop at the next exit to try and find out what on earth has
happened to my fuzzy lil' traveling companion.

Never did find it. But I sure did get plenty of water to wash my
mouth out, and a burger to try and create some new aftertaste. How
on earth a creeper could get into a vacuum-sealed package—let
alone stay *alive* without oxygen—is something I will never be able
to figure out. Also... did I ingest part of the critter or perhaps some
of its eggs? My mouth gets clammy just thinking about it. Needless
to say, I have never stopped at a Stuckey's ever again. And I now
examine all pre-wrapped foods carefully before sticking them in my
mouth.

CHAPTER 16

I SHOULDA KISSED HER

For some odd reason the name Michelle seems to have a special draw on me. Maybe it's due to lithe Michelle O. who was our next door neighbor and my sister's best friend during our elementary years. We used to serenade her with: "Michelle, My Belle" by the Beatles, while she went through her ballet poses. It wasn't just a passing phase; she ended up dancing professionally for several large ballet companies and owns her own studio to this day.

There was the brunette Michelle at Eisenhower High, a willowy beauty at Wheaton College, and a blonde with the cutest bob hairdo while living in Nashville—all Michelles. There was "the tall one with the entrancing eyes" that began as a blind date in Colorado while I was visiting from Tennessee... which evolved over the following eight months into a few deep discussions about marriage. Alas; long distance romances have rarely worked in my experience.

But it was Michelle K.—who I met a few years after getting my degree—who can still capture my thoughts on occasion, even two decades later. Initially, I was head-over-heels for her sister, Melody. We had met at a singles class in at Winnetka Bible Church, in the northern 'burbs of Chicago. She had that natural beauty radiating from her genuine smile that was framed by thick, cascading black locks a la Andie MacDowell. But Melody's true attraction was her sincerity and gentle kindness. So easy to speak with… so interested in others. We spoke often, and I was beginning to think something was building between us.

She had briefly mentioned a guy named Steve living in Michigan, but I had no idea how close they were until she returned from a weekend trip beaming with joy. He had proposed out of the blue, and she accepted, showing everyone at our Tuesday evening support group the lovely engagement ring. I put on a good front, but my heart was sinking like a sack full of horseshoes in Hudson Bay.

In the following months, Melody and I continued to interact, and I eventually met Steve, who turned out to be an absolutely "Grade A" guy. He and I became basketball buddies whenever he came to visit and have remained great friends to this day.

From time to time, Melody would mention her kid sister, Michelle, who was in her freshman year at Northern Illinois University. She would solicit prayers for her, because "Mick"—as she was known to her family—was going through a lot of temptations common for young students at a party school… and NIU was known far and wide as just that.

Because the guys in Kansas were friends of mine; when Melody heard that they were coming to NIU for a show, she wondered if we could get some free passes to meet with the band. You see, one of the other members, Dave Hope, had also become a Christian, and whenever they were within four hours of Chitown, they liked for me to try and get some other believers rounded up for fellowship and prayer after the concert. Melody knew of these get-togethers and thought Michelle might garner some incentive in her faith from that atmosphere.

So Melody and I made the two-hour trip out to DeKalb. I couldn't help but notice how stunning she was: if anything, even more be-atific now that she was deeply committed to Steve and glowing in that mutual assurance. I kept reminding myself that I should be welcoming of that relationship—and certainly not pining away for someone who was so obviously smitten in the best sense of the word. Several times during the drive, she mentioned how Michelle was looking forward to meeting me (I guess Mel had been "talking me up" to her). But I sort of scoffed at the idea internally. I mean, who could *possibly* be more intriguing than the woman sitting in my passenger seat?

Once we arrived at the arena, Kerry invited us to have dinner with them backstage. So Mel called her sister with directions on where to meet us. Being a big arena rock show, there were dozens of nubile young ladies circulating in and around the dressing room and catering areas. The Kansas guys were all happily married and this had little effect on them. However, the up and coming Loverboy was opening on this tour, and they were having lots of jollies with all these "Hot Girls In Love."

As Kerry was leading us to dine, one young woman held my gaze, as well as the attention of most of the other men within eyeshot. She exuded a certain grace as she walked in, her effervescent smile melting all that came in its range. She was searching for someone, and with a gleam in her eye, she started heading in our general di-rection. Imagine my amazement when she and Mel embraced, and her sister said, "Mick, this is my friend I've been telling you about: Mark." It was like when Garth first saw Donna Dixon in *Wayne's World*, except exponentially better. I had something much more than just a "schwiiiing!" incident... There was something shimmer-ing deep in the recesses of my heart.

We hit it off immediately. Despite her beauty, she was very easy to converse with, just like her sister. The concert in the basketball arena was brilliant: made even more so by the band seating us in the first row. The ensuing fellowship time, with a dozen other believers sharing and praying in an unused football team shower room, was kinetic. Michelle was luminous... glowing from the excitement of it all.

Over the next few weeks, Melody mentioned to me several times that Michelle was asking about me in their phone calls and suggested I call her. There was palpable synergy between us when I did. Michelle came home on Spring break, and we got together several times, including a visit to the aforementioned support group that Mel and I were in. During sharing time, Michelle beamed how this would become her spiritual home when she got home for the summer and how much she had been enjoying the calls and letters I'd been sending that meant so much to her.

The next few month's communiqués and occasional weekend visits were wonderful. We were developing a strong friendship based on mutual encouragement and prayer. It grew even deeper when May rolled around and she came back to Chicago for the mid-year break. When we weren't together at a movie, concert, church, restaurant, Bible study, or hanging out at each other's homes, we were on the phone. We'd have these amazing talks and prayer times together.

One night at our cell group meeting, we were playing a group encounter board game, and she landed on a space called: "Do Your Own Thing," where you could say anything that was on your heart. Michelle wasn't particularly shy, and she looked directly at me and said, "This has been the most wonderful time getting to know you Mark, and I'm looking forward to even more." This elicited some sideways glances toward me from others in the group, as if to say, *Well, whaddya know—Mark and Michelle are an item!*

Everyone knew that I had been praying dutifully about the area of relationships and that I was earnestly seeking God's will for a mate. This was a very open fellowship, so everyone shared each other's struggles in dealings with the opposite sex and how we wanted to be accountable. Michelle and I had been reading Watchman Nee and A.W. Tozer, and we were resonating with their instructions on striving for holiness.

Did I mention that Michelle was (and is) an utter knockout? Her shimmering hazel green eyes, sunny smile, and tan face were perfectly framed by flowing light brown hair that fell like a breeze on and around her shoulders. Her great culinary habits and physical acumen kept her body in fantastic shape. She didn't need to wear much makeup or jewelry, but when she did, it augmented her attributes impeccably. And, just like her older sister, she had an incredibly gracious soul.

On several get-togethers, we would look longingly at each other, only to kind of stammer and say, "Well, we'd better be careful." Hence; even though we were both fairly eaten up with the idea of holding hands, caressing, and (dare I say it?) kissing, we always somehow managed to control our glandular motives. How strange it was to have our hearts and conversations so open... so close that we would actually confess to one another that we were having lustful thoughts toward the other, and would the other be able to forgive us—despite never acting on those thoughts. In committing to this reverence toward each other, we denied any level of physical intimacy. It was, in a word, insanity. Our super-spirituality was ultimately our undoing.

For several months, I had been debating a possible move away from Chicago. I had eight job offers that included cool opportunities in the music biz in Nashville. Michelle and I had invested hours and hours of prayer together on this subject alone. We felt that God had brought us together in this very special friendship, but we also knew His plans were the most important—and not how we felt. In early July, I sensed several confirmations leading me to accept one of the positions at a record label in Tennessee, and a few hours later, I expressed that with the support group in our weekly meeting. As I shared with my closest friends where I thought God was leading me—and the words: "I think I'm supposed to move to Nashville"—came out of my mouth, I saw Michelle's eyes fill up, and tears start to roll down her cheeks... the cheeks that I had longed to hold against mine.

As the group was separating later that evening, Mick and I chatted briefly... and awkwardly. Hours later, at nearly midnight, I called her because my heart was heavy. She couldn't sleep either. We spoke well into the wee hours of the morning. We were being mutually benevolent and speaking wonderful hope into each other's hearts about what God had in store for us individually. But we were still hesitant to admit the fear that being apart would hinder something very, very special between us.

In the subsequent weeks leading up to my departure, we continued to invest tremendously into each other. More time-transcendent prayers. A couple of wonderful picnics. A hilarity-filled day at Great America Amusement Park. Deep, soul-stirring and filling conversations. Lots of laughter. A few tears. But still, we fought the temptation to be physical.

Upon my arrival in Nashville, we spoke habitually on the phone and wrote lengthy letters. But it was evident that something was missing. I returned north for a visit a month later, and there was some strain as we were together. In fact, we had our first argument. I have no recollection what it was about, but the memory still stings.

We both continued to pray passionately about how God was leading us... but just too timid to express ourselves in open affection.

Eventually Michelle met a guy at NIU later that fall, and they became involved. I ended up leaving the record company, but I stayed in Nashville managing Petra—whose career was exploding—and averaged about eighty hours a week working on their hugely successful *More Power To Ya* album and adjoining tour. But despite the hyperactivity, I missed her deeply. I regularly had dreams about her (one of the few women that has ever captured me in that way), and when I'd allow myself the time, I could pine away with intense sadness over what could have been.

As the years unfolded, Michelle and I remained dear friends. She went through some other relationships. I would become occupied with other women as well... but for many years, every single lady I would spend time with was judged on my internal "Michelle Scale"... and they always came up short (I know that this was patently unfair to these lovely women, and I know that it didn't help any potential we might have had).

Michelle finished her undergrad degree and worked her way through medical school. Eventually, she married a terrific gentleman name Mike who is a combo lawyer and United Airlines pilot. They have two lovely toe-headed kids now, and Mick has become a highly-sought-after surgeon in Chicago. They both have a strong desire to help the less fortunate and work at making their faith a relevant part of their lives.

We still chat on the phone from time to time and see each other whenever possible if I'm in Chicago. On a couple of occasions, we have wistfully reminisced about those months when we had first met. I recall one long phone call about fifteen years ago when—after poking some fun at our zeal to be so spiritually pure in our relationship—Michelle paused and said, "You know, Mark, if we had just kissed, then we would probably be married now."

I sighed my agreement. "Yeah... you're probably right... What were we so scared of?" We both chuckled softly. "My, oh my... was I ever in love with you," I lamented.

"Yeah... me, too," she whispered. There was another long pause, and we then sheepishly moved into other areas on which we needed to catch-up with each other.

In no way whatsoever am I lobbying or even longing for some sort of renewal between us. Our lives have both led us into areas where we have been greatly blessed and have allowed us to give liberally to others. We are both happy for each other and still garner great satisfaction in seeing how the other's life has unfolded.

But here I sit during another Valentine's week, pondering what might have been with various liaisons I've had along my journey. Certainly I've had my portion of romantic love. And yes, my libido has gotten out of control—most of the time with women I have cared deeply for—but even the sundry one night stand. In all the cases, it was mutually desired and satisfying in its own way I suppose. Perhaps in those instances, I was "acting out" on what I felt I had missed with Michelle.

I've admitted, confessed, and asked forgiveness where I was wrong in these encounters. Just as I try to not wallow in regret over sins of the flesh, I also try not to beat myself up over my and Michelle's self-imposed reverential restrictions all those years back.

But... I still sometimes wonder... and think to myself... *I shoulda just kissed her.*

CHAPTER 17

IF YOU REALLY WANNA DIE,
LET ME HELP YOU

Andy was drinking again. But this time it was worse... perhaps the worst yet. He was waving around a .357 magnum (yeah, the "Do you feel lucky, punk?" model) that he had gotten God-knows-where. In his drunken stupor, he even showed me that it was fully loaded.

"I'm sick of my shitty life!" he yelled. "I'm sick of a goulish God who let me get this way... and I'm sick of cocky Christians like you who don't give a rat's ass," he slurred as he recklessly pointed the weapon in my direction.

Andy had been my roommate, along with Bob and Brian, for the past couple years. We knew when he joined us that he had some severe difficulties, though we agreed to help him work through them... but I never thought it would come to this.

I met him at a church singles picnic. Because of his severe facial disfigurement, he was being pretty much universally ignored by the over 100 in attendance, including me. After about an hour of interacting with many others—but watching him out of the corner of my eye—my guilt, as well as my curiosity, got the best of me.

After introducing myself, I asked him if he liked softball and if he'd like to join in a pick-up game. Despite the fact that he had been chain-smoking the entire time, he turned out to be a pretty decent athlete. When the game was completed, I grabbed a couple of 7-Ups and we sat down away from the rest of the group.

It was odd, but I felt the same resolve in looking directly at him that I had when I was bold enough to ask out the prettiest girl at Wheaton College: the incomparable Lisa Avis. She absolutely melted me and every other guy on campus with her eyes. She was the hottest freshman in the whole school, and that was agreed-upon by any red-blooded male. But I boldly asked her out over the phone and vowed that I would not veer my gaze away from hers on that first lunch date. I determined to do the same now with Andy.

The entire left side of his face was caved-in and discolored from numerous surgeries. He was missing many of the teeth on that side of his mouth, and his lips contorted in such a way that when he spoke, it was often difficult to understand him, initially. The pinkish surgical scars also ran from behind his left ear, down his neck, and under what was left of his chin. I've often felt that when there is an elephant in the room, you might as well talk about it instead of trying to act as if it didn't exist. "If you don't mind me asking, Andy, what happened to your face?"

A sly grin came over him, and there was a twinkle in his eye. "I've been coming to this church for three weeks now... and you're the first person who has actually asked me," he laughed. He paused to light another in the non-stop parade of Marlboro Reds. Taking a long drag, he stared off, exhaled, and began his sad tale.

Andy came from a well-to-do family in Glenview, in Chicago's wealthy northern suburbs. In his teens, he got mixed up with the wrong crowd and began coking and drinking heavily. He felt that getting loaded made him feel wittier with his friends, and it helped assuage the pain he felt from his dysfunctional home. But what was initially an escape had evolved into addiction, and as he grew angry and unstable with his condition, his social circle began to avoid him. Suicidal thoughts started to surface.

One night, during a particularly nasty binge, he got his father's shotgun, managed to wedge it under his jaw, and pulled the trigger. The blast didn't wake anyone in the house because he was usually playing insanely loud music in his soundproofed room, and it must've blended in with the thumping.

Andy took another long pull on his cigarette. "You know the weirdest thing, Mark? I was so screwed-up from booze and who-knows-what-else I inhaled that night, that I had lousy aim—or at least was off by just a few inches. I could barely feel what I had done. Most anyone would've been knocked out, but I was wide awake. Blood was everywhere, and I immediately knew I was in serious trouble. I stumbled up the stairs at 1 AM and burst into my parent's room incomprehensibly screaming, with half of my face hanging off: some remnants of facial muscles keeping what was left of my jaw in place. I was rushed to the hospital, where they operated on me for six hours. Over the next week, there were several more surgeries. Most doctors felt I wasn't going to make it."

Between puffs on his cig, Andy would intermittently look at me; I suppose wondering when I would check out and make some lame excuse and get up to leave. But I was determined to look at him squarely and to keep listening—you know, the Lisa Avis resolve and all.

That crooked, knowing smile that I would come to know well, came over his face again, and he continued. I could tell this was good for him—he didn't get to share this very often, and he told me so.

Over the next month in that hospital ICU, he prayed that God would let him die numerous times. He recalled one woman who stopped by to visit and pray with him. He didn't know her from Eve. But she gave him a Bible, and out of sheer boredom one long evening, he started reading it, thinking maybe he needed to try and understand God a little better before getting out of the hospital and finally finishing the job he had so poorly started.

But something happened one dark night of the soul as he cried out in his pain and loneliness to Jesus. He began to feel strangely warmed and accepted. Without anyone else's prompting, he decided to give his life over to God.

None of his "friends" came to visit him. His family felt ashamed and awkward because of what he had done to himself, and Andy knew he was gonna be on his own—at least psychologically. Being sober for a month while in that hospital brought back his love for reading, and he voraciously devoured the scriptures as well as other Christian books. His parents were agnostics, and while they were glad that Andy was finding some peace, he thought they were perturbed about his newfound serenity. After all, they were going to have to shoulder what was going to become a costly ordeal in his recovery.

Months segued into years. At least a dozen more surgeries were performed trying to rebuild Andy's dental work, jaw, and various skin grafts. I can't begin to imagine how painful this was for him physically, but even more so, emotionally and spiritually. He grew tremendously in his faith; yet, due to his appearance, he lacked confidence in trying to mix socially. He admitted that he would sometimes fall off the wagon and drink heavily, trying to self medicate his emotional pain. One of those instances got his license revoked for driving under the influence. But he had built a small house painting business, and his employees would meet him each morning and drive to each job in his van.

Several times each year, he would try to enter into fellowship, but those he met in churches tended to avoid him... make him feel unwanted. But he would regroup after each cycle of feeling alienated and try again.

So, it was eight years after his suicide attempt. Our conversation lasted deep into the afternoon. Most everyone was leaving the picnic when we realized how long we had been talking. I told Andy about the small Bible study I helped lead and asked if he would like to come. Taking a final puff, he dropped the butt at his feet and began snuffing the ember out with his shoe. "Really? I mean... really?" There was awful apprehension in his voice. He didn't want to feel rejected yet again.

"Sure," I replied.

I picked him up that Wednesday. That began a great relationship. Andy became a regular in that small support group. Eventually, as Brian and Bob got to know Andy as well, we decided to ask him to move into the spare room in the basement. It would be the first time he ever lived outside of his parents' home.

Andy blossomed in this new environment. He launched into redecorating what was once a dingy laundry room into a cool domicile. Turns out he was a pretty good cook, too. And because he had read so much in his self-imposed reclusion over the years, he was a great conversationalist on any number of topics. He had been a good athlete in his high school days and had kept himself in good shape with lots of sit-ups and push-ups. So sometimes we would work out together as well as play some baseball and basketball. When you get to know someone, you get used to everything about them. It got to the point where I never even noticed his scars.

When Andy put his mind to something, he was amazing. He decided to start investing in the stock market and got fairly good at it. I remember one evening when he had timed a buy and turnaround just perfectly and had made thousands of dollars in a matter of hours. He celebrated by preparing an amazing feast for the rest of us: prime rib, au gratin potatoes, and steamed avocadoes in melted butter.

Another time, he decided he wanted to learn to play piano, so he bought a beat up baby grand that had been covered in green house paint and refurbished it completely on his own. The refinished wood alone looked amazing. When it came time to put the legs back on it, he couldn't wait for the other three of us to get home from work, so he somehow managed to lift the 500-pound instrument on his own and get all three legs screwed into place. I still have no idea how he did it. He then proceeded to self-teach—and became proficient.

When Andy moved in, we all knew there would be risks. He openly admitted that he would still sometimes get drunk. We agreed to rid the house of any alcohol and that we would do everything in our power to help him stay clean and sober. Despite our best efforts, every few months, Andy would somehow get a hold of some whisky and get plastered. Normally, he was a quiet drunk, and we could help him mellow out over the course of a day or two, and then he'd refocus and move onward. Sometimes he would get pretty angry about his predicament and launch into diatribes about wanting to "off himself."

Over the years, Andy had begun reading many of the "prosperity gospel" teachings by people like Ken Hagen, Robert Tilton, Oral Roberts, Kenneth Copeland, and that ilk. These scoundrels have somehow managed to take selective portions of the Bible and twist them to appear that God wants everyone to be wealthy and healthy all the time. This warped teaching postulates that if anyone is not rich and is suffering from some ailment, then there must be a lack of faith on their part compromising God's promises. That shortcoming can only be overcome by giving a "faith gift" to God (usually in the form of a big donation to their particular ministry) that will prove to God that you are serious. Only by giving sacrificially will God be willing to give you all the desires of your heart. If there is some lack in your life, then you simply haven't sewn enough faith into it and need to give more. It's a vicious and evil cycle that is an insult to everything that Christ taught and exemplified... and has led to great financial and spiritual ruin for nearly everyone that I have seen enter into it. Fortunately, most people see the fault in it, eventually (and in themselves for being drawn to it)—but there is usually some deep anguish along the way.

Andy and I would have some pretty strong discussions—even arguments—about this. My involvement with Christians who were desperately poor in the developing world had clearly shown me that this uniquely American upper-middle class aberration of scripture was just plain wrong-headed. God loves us all, no matter what our condition. He isn't embarrassed or emasculated somehow if we aren't always living in prosperity. If anything, it is our wrestling with pain and difficulty that produces character and allows God to teach us so much more about life.

But the ache and scars of Andy's poor decision eight years earlier were often overwhelming. He felt such tremendous remorse, and the proof of it stared him in the mirror every morning. In his most delusional moments, he would tell me that God had indeed healed him but that it just hadn't been manifested yet. With each passing day, that realization would haunt him—even taunt him—further.

So, here we were on a stormy Saturday night. Brian was home

visiting with his family in central Illinois, and Bob had gone hunting in Wisconsin. It was just me, Andy, and his massive handgun that he was waving about recklessly. His temper would begin to rage at times, and he would actually cock the hammer and place it to his temple saying, "No more jackin' around. I'm gonna fuckin' do it right this time!" Then he would laugh or point the gun at me, accusing me of trying to sabotage his faith. "You're making me feel like a dirt bag before God!"

I've come to discover over the years that reasoning with a drunk or someone who is stoned is like trying to negotiate with a petulant three-year-old. I have little time for it, and yet, here I was again, dealing with someone who was not in his right mind. I say 'again', because I had to deal with my acid-tripping brother sometimes or my alcoholic grandfather. The latter had ruined his family over many years of gambling and booze. The impact of his problems was far-reaching for years afterwards. As a result, my mother had no tolerance whatsoever for anything that even hinted of alcohol, and I guess it got passed along to me. I helped clean Grandpa up on several occasions, and it sickened me. But he never improved, and I was the one that found him dead in his apartment bathroom floor from a drunken binge that had led to a massive heart attack.

Andy was really plastered, and he kept sipping from a bottle of Jim Beam, all the while keeping a firm grip on the weapon. Between rants, he would sit across from me, and I would try to help him think through all that he had accomplished, all that God had helped him with. A few times the tears would begin to well up, and he would admit to his own responsibility. But then he would begin agonizing over his shame, his frustration with God for allowing it to happen, and with Jesus for not healing him, and the anger would swell again. This went on for three hours, with each round getting worse. I was getting concerned that he was at a true breaking point.

Praying for guidance in the midst of a situation like this can be hard. But eventually I recalled a particular episode of *M.A.S.H.* I had seen the year before, where Colonel Potter had an intense confrontation with a drunken, suicidal soldier who was recovering from wounds that were going to leave him crippled for life. Could I have the guts to try what I saw on that TV show? Another couple cycles of Andy's rage and remorse convinced me that I had to give it a try— things might take a much uglier turn if I didn't do *something.*

Andy had just had the gun in his mouth and was babbling about what his brains might look like blown all over the ceiling. As he finally let the gun down and began taking another draw from his bottle, I lunged across the table. I had completely caught him off guard, and I yanked the heavy handgun away from him while wrestling him to the floor.

I was straddled across his chest, with my left arm across his throat. Taking the pistol, I held it to his temple and yelled, "You know, I'm sick of this B.S., Andy! If you want to die so badly, let me take the pressure off and do it for you! I'm going to blow your decrepit brains out. I won't be accused of murder, because I could claim self defense from your drunken tirade!" Andy was choking and struggling and started to protest.

"I'm as serious as a fuckin' siezure, Andy! If you want to end it, I will gladly pull this trigger! You wanna die so badly; let me help you… Let's quit screwin' around!"

I pressed the barrel firmly against his skull. "You ready? 'Cause here goes!"

Andy was squirming wildly and began screaming, "I don't wanna die! I don't wanna die! Don't kill me!"

"Why should I believe you?!" I yelled. "You keep pulling this horse crap on yourself and the rest of us. I don't want to deprive you of your sick sense of self-loathing. It's getting way too old, and it's time for your stupid life to come to an end!" I put even more pressure on his neck and pulled the hammer back with my thumb.

As he heard that ominous click, Andy began sobbing, "Please don't kill me! I don't wanna die!"

"What do you want to do, then?!" I demanded.

"I wanna live... I don't wanna die," he choked between gasps, gurgling tears and snot.

I let the pressure off the hammer and slid the gun into the kitchen along the floor. I eased off his chest, leaned against the wall and pulled Andy up as he cried deeply. He slumped against me, and I put my arm around him. Between his heaving shudders, he wrapped his arms around me and sobbed heavily into my shoulder. I rocked him gently. He was nearly passed out from the ordeal. I don't think I've ever felt someone weep so intensely.

After a few minutes, I asked if he wanted to sober up. He agreed, and I helped lead him up the stairs to the bathroom, where I stood him in the shower and ran lukewarm water over him in his whisky-stenched clothes. He started to vomit, so I sat him down in the tub and helped him as he purged.

Later, after changing him into some dry clothes and serving him several strong cups of coffee, I negotiated him into his bed.

I removed the bullets from the heavy handgun and tossed them down a sewer, then wrapped the pistol in some old rags and threw it into one of the dumpsters out back.

The next morning, Andy had a horrible case of the D.T.'s and threw up a few more times. Eventually, he got a bit of an appetite, and we went out to eat, where he began to speak of how he was going to be even more determined on trying to get past his drinking and his self-destructive tendencies. But we also talked with much accomplishment about how far he had come and where he was headed.

As the months moved forward, Andy began weaning himself from the "name it and claim it" teachings that did little more than make him feel inadequate.

Andy and I never spoke of the gun incident again. We didn't have to.

I eventually relocated to Nashville and Andy helped with the move. He came to visit several times. Whenever I would head back to Chicago, I looked forward to seeing him there, too. We shared many long phone calls, sometimes even when he was drunk on occasion—such is the pernicious disease of alcoholism. But I never heard him talk about ending his life ever again since that dark night. He was a fighter. And despite the self-inflicted burden he carried, Andy moved on in his life with God's help, forgiveness, and a big supply of hope.

CHAPTER 18

THE FIRST TIME I MET U2

W as December sixth, 1981 just shortly after their *October* album had been released. They were early into their second U.S. tour, returning to Chicago's famed Park West nightclub where they had played less than a year before in support of their debut, *Boy*.

That initial album was sonically and emotionally intriguing, but it was quite difficult to surmise what the lyrics were about, due to the heavy reverb on Bono's voice and his thick Irish brogue, not to mention the rather vague imagery. But I had heard from Terry Taylor of Daniel Amos that they were Christians and that I should check them out. The overall soundscape they created was mesmerizing, and I was becoming a fan.

When their sophomore effort was released, all doubt about their faith was quickly erased. Nearly every cut on *October* was full of Biblical imagery, praise toward God and goodness, and a profound sense of battling one's own sin. Since they were still an obscure entity, there was very little press or interviews to glean more info from. But I was immersed in the album, and it helped bring some focus to the tunes from the first project.

I was dating a lovely British girl named Wendy at the time. She was in the States as a nanny for some friends of her family, and we had met at my church. I found her accent and coy smile enchanting but was drawn toward her thoughtful honesty as much as anything. We quickly found we could share about deeper issues, having discovered that we had both suffered from some painful losses in recent years.

One of the reasons she had come stateside was to try to work through the grief of her father's death in a plane crash. She was wrestling with many hard doubts about why God would allow such a thing to happen. Since I had delved in similar despair from losing those friends during my college years, I was more than willing to allow her pained questions and sorrow in many a long conversation.

Like me, she was resonating with the naked confessions of Bono when she heard me playing the albums. Wendy had become aware of the U2 buzz that was building in England that summer, so she was keen on the idea of coming with me to the show.

As a rock journalist, I was able to get passes to any concert I wanted, and my representative from Island Records was eager to get industry insiders to come out and experience what some already knew was something very magical. He invited us to come to the after-show party as well.

Having developed some friendships over the years with other thoughtful Christians in the music world, like Bruce Cockburn, Dave Pack from Ambrosia, Paul Goddard from Atlanta Rhythm Section, Richie Furay from Poco/Buffalo Springfield, and others, I felt an ease in being able to chat in normal terms about faith in the rock 'n' roll world. I decided to put together a "care package" of cool albums by artists who were Christians that might be of encouragement to these youngsters from Dublin. It included *Stop the Dominos* by Mark Heard, *Alarma* by Daniel Amos, *Zionic Bonds* by Andy McCarroll, and

Moral Support (an Irish punk band from Belfast), as well as *Humans* and *Inner City Front* by the aforementioned Cockburn.

From the moment the lights dimmed in the 700-seat club, Wendy and I knew we were indeed in for something special. Even at this embryonic stage of their development, U2 had a flair for the dramatic. They hired a local Irish bagpipes corps to march in, blaring out the familiar strains of "Amazing Grace." The shaggy haired quartet followed them down the aisles and leapt onto the stage, with Larry Mullen pounding out the opening drum beat to "Gloria," and all heaven broke loose when Bono, Edge, and Adam Clayton all joined in on the downbeat. On the huge chorus, the sixteen-foot-high lighting rig of mostly white beams was fully lit, revealing its shape as a huge cross.

During the guitar lead, Bono walked out onto several of the tables that were huddled on the main floor and grabbed someone's glass of water. When he balanced his way back to the stage, just at the crescendo of Edge's sonic assault, he tossed the contents of the glass high above himself, then opened his arms, arched his back, and soaked in the cascading baptism of life-giving fluid with a huge smile on his face. The packed house roared, and with fists pumping and everyone pogoing to the manic beat, we were singing full throat this song of passionate surrender. This was no reactionary, sullen punk band. This was something quite different... fresh... relevant. No cynicism, but still plenty of rock swagger. No pointless angst, but scads of emotional and spiritual release. I think everyone sensed that something very great was being birthed in these spotty-faced teenagers from the Emerald Isle.

As the concert progressed, Bono continued to break down that imaginary wall that often keeps the audience and the performer from connecting. Even at this young age of twenty-one, he had such command of each unfolding situation and was fully alive within that given moment. On their final song, a rough version of "40" that would appear the following year on their *War* album—Bono took one of the thousand-watt par lights, hoisted it on his shoulder, and took his time shining the intense shaft on the face of each and every one of us who were in the audience. Then, as he does even to this day, he placed the light on the floor, turned the beam straight up, and the group left the stage one by one as the song was deconstructed down to the stark drum beat.

Wendy and I looked at each other as the gathering cheered. All we could say was, "Wow!"

After the crowd began to disperse, we made our way back to the tiny backstage green room area. We were invited in by my record label buddy, and there must've been fifty people packed into the space of a normal-sized bedroom. You could barely move, but there was a joyous sense of anticipation amongst all of us wanting to congratulate the band on such a powerful performance. Bono already knew how to "work a room" and was incredibly gracious and focused with everyone he met. I waited for some of the throng to thin out a bit when I felt there would be a better chance to visit and give him the gifts.

When I introduced Wendy and myself, he was so warm, reaching out to shake our hands and repeating our names back to us several times as we chatted. He was enamored with the Irish history that was so prevalent in Chicago, He knew some Hollingsworth's in Ireland and wondered if I was from their brood. I told him there were lots of Russell's on my father's side of the family as well, and he was thrilled, since that is most definitely a Gaelic clan.

Bono noticed that I had a bunch of albums under my arm, and he said, "What do you have there, Mark?"

"Having listened to your lyrics quite a bit from your first two records, I thought you might enjoy these," I responded. I then told him a little about each artist, without coming right out and explaining that they were all men of faith. He was curiously looking over the song titles and even reading a few of the verses on the enclosed lyric sheets. In all my years of mingling with music personalities, I have always taken time, over the course of several interviews and meetings, before entering into a discussion of faith. It never felt right to be blunt. I mean, I wouldn't do it with any normal friendship, so why should I be pushy with strangers?

But for some odd reason, I felt compelled to be more direct with Bono than I had ever been with dozens of other artists in the past. Hesitating slightly, I then blurted out, "Bono, everything in your songs and your performances seem to point clearly in this direction, but I was just wondering if you could tell me if you guys are Christians?"

I'll never forget his response. He reached out and grabbed both of my shoulders, then looked sharply to his right and sharply to his left, as if to see if "the coast was clear" in a sort of mock fear. Then he looked me straight in the eyes and said, "We're secret agents!" And we both burst into fun, nudge-nudge kind of laughter.

Countering me, he then turned the tables. "How about you; are you a Christian?"

"Why yes, I am," I happily confessed. "That's why I thought you'd find encouragement from these artists who are also working their way through hard questions of faith in their music."

"That's so cool!" He exclaimed. "How about you, Wendy?"

Before she could answer, he took both of our arms and said, "This is fantastic! Come with me," and he led us about ten feet through several clusters of people—over to Edge and Larry who were talking with some folks on the other side of the room.

Bono politely interrupted the chat that was going on and declared, "Sorry to barge in, but I wanted you guys to meet Mark and Wendy... They're believers, too!" It was suddenly like old home week, with Edge and Larry both pumping our hands, exclaiming, "Brilliant! We don't get to meet too many fellow believers when we're on the road." They took to Wendy immediately because of her accent. And they were thrilled to hear that she was from London, where they played quite often.

The three asked us where we went to church, and they shared a bit about the charismatic fellowship they were part of back in Dublin. I wondered if Adam Clayton was a Christian as well. "Nah... not yet, anyway." Edge smiled. Larry asked how long I had known the Lord, and I told him that I had been raised in the church but had my first strong commitment while I was in my teens, then another reawakening three years ago. He said it had been kind of the same with him. He then turned to my friend and said, "How about you, Wendy; how long have you known Jesus?"

To her credit—and this was one of the things I liked so much about her—she didn't give a pat answer. She paused, looked down at the floor in a bit of sadness, and said, "I'm not really sure what I believe right now. My Dad was killed last year, and I'm pretty angry with God."

You could see Larry's demeanor change. His shoulders drooped also; he sighed heavily, kind of harmonizing her pain. He then gently took her hand and said, "Can I show you something?" She looked at me for my approval, and I nodded, "Sure, go ahead."

He led her over to where there were two empty chairs; he sat down with her, and he pulled a Bible out of his shoulder bag. As Edge, Bono, and I kept chatting about the music scene in general and about the artists I had brought for them on those albums; out of the corner of my eye, I was watching what was transpiring with Wendy and Larry. I noticed that he was showing her lots of scriptures (she later told me they were encouraging passages from Isaiah and Psalms mostly: exhortations about the Lord hearing our laments and not forgetting us). After several minutes, I saw that he had his hand on her shoulder and was praying for her.

About that time, their road manager started clearing the room so they could get ready for an all-night bus ride to their next show. The drummer and Wendy rejoined our little conclave, and as we were saying our goodbyes, he asked if she would be back in London over the holidays. "Yes, I'll be back to visit with Mum and my family."

"Lovely!" Larry beamed. "Will you please come as my guest to our show at Lyceum Theater a few days before Christmas? I'll get everything squared away for you and anyone from your family who'd like to join you." He handed her a note that had several of the scripture references written on them, as well as their business card that she could contact for the tickets. "I'd love to see you again and hear how you are doing. I'll be praying for you, Wendy."

"Thanks again for the music, Mark," Bono and Edge chimed in. "Hopefully we'll get to see you and spend more time next time we're here." We were then politely ushered out with the last few stragglers.

Wendy was quite taken aback with the kindness of these strangers. It gave her much to think and contemplate about as she continued to work through her grief. And yes, as the Psalms say: eventually her mourning did turn into gladness, and she came back to a loving faith in God despite her profound loss.

A few months later, I got a nice postcard from the band. It read, "Mark! Thanks again for the great albums. We especially like the Bruce Cockburn! (signed) Bono, The Edge, Larry Mullen, Jr."

I still have that one in my collection.

And it was great to spend lots more time with them over the years after shows in Boston (*Unforgettable Fire* Tour), Denver (Amnesty International Tour and the tapings of the *Rattle and Hum* movie/CD), and Atlanta (Zoo TV Tour). Good lads, those boys.

CHAPTER 19

A Bellowing Babe and Handy Dandies over Cartagena

Being the Den Mother on dozens of overseas trips for bands and agencies that help the poor, I'm usually the first one up each morning and the last to bed each evening. In between I'm generally scurrying about behind the scenes trying to make sure all details are being taken care of. This helps lessen the culture shock and fatigue that most of my guests experience on these emotionally draining caravans. By the time our final day arrives and we are winging our way homeward, I am fairly exhausted and look forward to some extended sleep on the lengthy airline ride.

Having taken over 1,700 flights in my travels, I have grown accustomed to delays, lost luggage, and insensitive row mates. Rude ticket agents, malfunctioning conveyor belts, and unprepared gate attendants are more often than not the norm these days. I just suck it up and try to get on with what's been laid before me. After all, less than a hundred years ago, many of these journeys would've taken six weeks as opposed to a matter of a half day—so I try to put things in perspective while grinning and bearing it.

But allow me—just for fun—to vent a bit regarding a jaunt back to the States not long ago (sometimes cleansing one's bitter mind is good for the soul... or at least it feels like a quality poo).

The day began at 5:30 AM, after just five hours of sleep in the 7,500-foot-altitude air of central Colombia. Thirty minutes of closure to our five-day account at the front desk of the Hotel Capital went relatively smoothly. Our shuttle arrived on time, and we whisked through the quiet streets of this burgeoning metropolis of ten million souls to arrive at the Bogota Airport at 7:30. It's always good to allow at least three hours for check-in on this type of flight out of a developing nation... and, as it turned out, we were going to need every second of that allotment.

Never in my million-plus-miles of traversing the globe have I seen the bureaucratic imbroglio that is Bogota's international terminal. First, we got in a Delta ticket line that was easily the length of a football field... but then we were told we needed to move to another 150-foot line to register for exit tax exemption. So it was back to the Delta line, which—as it turns out—was really three sublines: a) to check-in our large luggage, b) to pay our government fees *again*, and c) to receive our seat assignments. Each of these took at least thirty minutes.

Then it was up several flights of stairs to another line, which would funnel us into the carry-on luggage x-ray screening, followed by another siphoning us through the customs departure procedure. Once each of us cleared that, there was another queue for individual bags to be opened and approved. We sauntered down the walkway to yet another 100-foot line in order to be admitted into our particular gate area, where we had to have our bodies and bags x-rayed *yet again.* Once in the gate area, we lined up to be allowed down the jet way, and we stood in line on that moving tunnel as everyone took their sweet time finding their seats, cramming their copious carry-ons into insufficient overhead and under-seat stowage.

All in all, it was eleven different lines, taking three hours and thirteen minutes. As one of my guests had declared, it was a dream job for some consultant to come in and figure out how to streamline "the Department of Redundancy Department" that had turned that terminal into a quagmire.

As I settled into my luxurious foot-and-a-half-wide seat, I realized that my six-foot, four-inch frame was going to have to accordion itself into legroom that even Verne Troyer would find oppressive. My plight was lessened by the gurgling joy of a twenty–month-old child two rows ahead of me who was wistfully jumping on her mother's lap, making playful eye contact with any who would engage her.

Lord knows I love children. Not only interacting playfully with those of my friends and relatives but also making them my life's work for sixteen years. Being an advocate for disadvantaged little ones brings about the deepest joy I know. So, when I explain what unfolded next, please grant me the latitude of an exhausted, sleep-deprived traveler whose last nerve was frayed like the strands on Charlie Daniels' fiddle bow.

Initially, this little tyke's infectious giggle was a respite for a weary soul. But over the next quarter of an hour, that waif evolved into a shrieking guttersnipe. No amount of hushing, threatening, or restraining from her frazzled mama, could quell this brazen brat. We can all identify the cries of a distressed infant in pain, and in most cases, we can tolerate such. But when a nipper is simply in a rebellious rant of Napoleonic proportions, we can all agree that it's as if Beelzebub's jaws came unhinged and one of his indigestible minions leapt out of his throat. Every half-minute or so, a wail that would make Geddy Lee cringe would then segue into a machine gun vibrato of sand-blasting intensity. This would only be quelled momentarily, then the imp would take a deep breath that would fuel the next round of audio excretion. Like I said, I felt like I had been "rode hard and put up wet," and her performance was the last thing I wanted to audition.

The thirty or so of us within immediate earshot all kept looking at each other with ever-widening eyes and that all-knowing nod as if to say, "I will stand in yet *another* line if it gives each of us the opportunity to jump off this jet and plunge seven miles to a relief only crushing death can bring!"

For decades I have proposed that airlines create a small, sound-proofed "cry room" for urchins like this and their distressed parent. A place where they can let it all hang out until their little lungs and willpower have nothing left to give, and they can then return in their weakened state to their seat. Or for large planes, even a sealed-off nursery area for multiple crybabies would be a blessing for all. However; on this particular day, I would've been happy if the mother had taken the little dickens to the lavatory, tied a rope around her, and flushed her out of the fuselage where she could dangle while decrying her fate. Hopefully, her little maw would freeze shut at 35,000 feet, and when she was pulled back thru the commode, it then might take the remainder of the flight for her high strung vocal chords to thaw out.

It was just a fleeting thought, though.

Even with this ongoing clatter, I was so tired that I began to nod into a half sleep, leaning my weary skull against the window frame. It was after far-too-short a respite that I was awakened by the elbow of the gentleman next to me. He was simply shifting his weight, but he didn't seem aware, let alone apologetic, that he had just gouged me with his bony joint. That was when I noticed that he and the man next to him were holding hands... not something you see every day on a sold-out flight and certainly not one originating in a highly Catholic third world country.

The guy immediately next to me was in his forties, with ruddy blonde hair and unkempt fingernails. His companion was considerably younger (early twenties I guessed), with smooth Colombian features, trendy black horn-rimmed glasses, and a red "Hitler Youth" t-shirt. When the older one spoke, his Spanish sounded forced through what appeared to be a Germanic accent. It was like hearing Colonel Klink with overly tight undergarments barking at suave Hispanic passers-by on South Beach. His partner was the more effeminate of the two and loved squeezing every ounce of sibilance out of any s-combos in his lexicon.

Trying to drift back into the nether world, I only got a few minutes of slumber before the atrocious tot from two rows up began another vile rendition of her iniquitous anthem. Moments turned into minutes. This diabolic cherub had made it her mission to ruin the bulk of the day for everyone, including—I'm convinced—any other aircraft jetting by within South American airspace at supersonic speeds.

But slumber finally befell me. At least until I was jostled again by the Aryan overlord, as he was reprimanding his companion in terse, guttural Spanish. Showing compliance, the younger of the two leaned heavily into his friend's chest and sighed deeply, while the other relented and kissed his neck.

My eyes rolled back into my skull as I leaned again into the crook of my seat and the wall. I was nearly delirious in my stupor. "I just wanna get some sleep!" I muttered to no one in particular.

Another explosive sequence from the reprobate bambino

aroused me just as lunch was to be served. While dining on dry chicken bits, soggy broccoli, and some sort of crumbling cheese paste, I observed the dandy duo cutting each other's meat, opening difficult bottle caps with dramatic flair, critiquing the culinary offerings with glee, and generally bickering like a retired Air Force couple.

Trying once more to nap after the meal, I was serenaded with another atrocious tirade from the Toddler of Horvath. This particular act of the opera lasted a good twenty minutes, but I somehow managed to find siesta.

My final awakening came when I heard deep moaning from my seatmate. Glancing downward, I saw that his consort had his hand down between the other's legs and was rubbing.

Get a room... or at least a blanket to cover yourselves, I thought. Coughing to let them know I was aware of their little display didn't seem to hinder their objective. I looked around to see if anyone else was privy to this show, but most everyone was either asleep or had their eyes glued to the monitors watching a movie with headphones blaring. Then I noticed that the elder was doing likewise manual gratification for his chum.

The temptation to ring my Flight Attendant button to turn in the loathsome lovers was strong. Perhaps they could be blasted by a fire extinguisher, in the same way my Dad used to douse two dogs in heat that were humping on our front lawn. In my drowsy state, I thought that might be the best course of action for this randy Rottweiler and his chummy Chihuahua.

Fortunately, before they could reach their "destination," the captain announced over the P.A. system that we were approaching Atlanta and that it was time to prepare the cabin for landing. They somehow focused on the task at hand (no, not *that* hand) and stopped their mutual pleasuring.

I shook my groggy head as we landed on the new south runway at Hartsfield International. This interminable excursion with the Nefarious Nina, Franz Fondelschlong, and his Colombian Queen, had finally come to an end.

CHAPTER 20

THE ETERNAL NOW

Praying for a stable mind
In the face of evil
I see people
Who are searching
For a sacred heart
That will last forever
Fail them never
Lasting contentment
Sure to remain
Ever unbroken
Ever the same

(David Sancious, "Ever the Same," from *True Stories*, 1978)

At times in my spiritual journey, I have found myself questioning certain aspects of God's omniscience. How can God be both eternal and temporal (as in the life of Christ)? How does God transcend time as we understand it? By being eternal, does God determine all events if He knows what their outcomes will be?

I've come to get a glimpse into how some of this may be an-

swered in the concept of "the eternal now." Great Christian thinkers like Augustine and Luther grappled with this outlook, but it
was Einstein's theory of relativity that helped put legs on it. Within
this paradigm, the faster you travel, the more time is compressed.
In laymen's terms, the theory goes something like this: If you were
to travel in a spaceship in a loop out beyond our solar system at
180,000 mph—and you returned in one hour—everything else
on earth would have aged a year. If you sped it up to 184,000 mph
and returned in an hour, everything would've aged 1,000 years. At
185,000 mph, the difference would be a million years. If you hit the
speed of light (186,000 mph), by the time you returned, the earth
might not even exist anymore... Time as we understand it wouldn't
mean anything.

The movie *Contact* touches on this issue. If Eleanor Arroway
(Jodie Foster's character) was traveling at the speed of light, she
might head out to another galaxy in that contraption the aliens
instructed the earthlings to build. However; the fear of Palmer
Ross—the minister who loved her (played by Matthew McCo-
noughey)—was that when she'd return, everyone else would be old
or gone altogether, yet she would still be the same age.

Isn't it interesting that God is referred to as Light in scripture
from the beginning in Genesis (1:1-4) through the end of Revelation (22:5)? Different versions of Light are used nearly 300 times in
the Bible. The reason why this is significant is this: At the speed of
light, time as we know it... time as a linear progression... does not
exist.

That's why the name of God is: "I Am that I Am." God always re-
fers to Himself in the present tense. When Moses asked the entity
in the burning bush to identify itself, it said, "I Am" (Exodus 3:14).
When the Pharisees questioned Christ about whether he had communicated with Abraham, Christ said, "Before Abraham was, I Am"

(John 8:58). That was either poor grammar on his part, or he was saying something quite profound... echoing the words of his Father. God never was. God never will be. God cannot be found in the past—or the future. He can only be found *now*. "I am the alpha and the omega... the beginning AND the end" (Revelation 1:8; 21:6; 22:13). God is now. "For me, time shall be no more" (Revelation 10:6).

Before the foundation of the earth—and this moment—and the end of the world—are all occurring NOW, to God. Everything is simultaneous. Augustine put it this way: "Before time, there is only eternity, and eternity for God is a never-ending present. For God, one day is like a thousand years, and a thousand years are like a day (II Peter 3:8)."

Once this is understood, we have a very interesting situation on our hands. Does God know before I'm ever born what I'm going to be and what I'm going to do? The answer is *Yes* and *No*. Yes from my point of view, because from my perspective, there is a before and an after. But with God, He doesn't know what's going to happen before it happens, because there is no before and there is no after with Him. So when we ask, "Does God know what I'm going to do before I do it?" there are two answers: If you're asking *me*, the answer is Yes; if you're asking *God*, the answer is No... because there's a historical and trans-historical approach to reality.

Philip Yancey uses this example:

> On the night of February twenty-third, 1987, an astronomer in Chile observed with his naked eye the explosion of a distant supernova: a blast so powerful that it released as much energy in one second as our sun will release in ten billion years. But did that event truly occur on February twenty-third, 1987? Only from our perspective, on our planet. Actually, the supernova exploded 170,000 years

prior to our 1987, but the light generated by that faraway event—traveling almost six trillion miles a year—took 170,000 years to reach our galaxy.

This is where the "higher view" of eternity defies our understanding of time. Imagine if you will, a very large Being, larger than the entire universe—so large that the Being exists simultaneously on earth and in the space occupied by Supernova 1987A. In 1987, what time was it for the Being? It depends on the perspective. From the perspective of earth, the being would have observed the 1987 history, which included the discovery of Supernova 1987A. But from the perspective of Supernova 1987A, the Being also would have experienced what the earth will not know for another 170,000 years! The Being thus observed both the past (from the earth, he saw the supernova explosion of 170,000 years before), the present (the events of 1987 on earth), and the future (what was happening on Supernova 1987A "now" that earthlings will not learn about for 170,000 years)... all simultaneously.

Such a Being, big as the universe, could—from some lookout post—see what is happening anywhere in the universe at any given time. For example; if he wants to know what is taking place on our sun right now, he can "watch" from the perspective of the sun. If he wants to see what took place on the sun eight minutes ago, he can "watch" from earth—that's what we see after light has traveled ninety-three million miles from the sun to earth.

C.S. Lewis writes:

If you picture Time as a straight line along which we have to travel, then you must picture God as the whole page on which the line is drawn. We come to parts of the line one-by-one: We have to leave A behind before we get to B, and we cannot reach C until we leave B behind. God—from above, or outside, or all around—contains the whole line and sees it all.

In *Slaughterhouse Five*, Kurt Vonnegut Jr. muses on this concept through the experiences of his universe-hopping character, Billy Pilgrim, who was for a time incarcerated in a human zoo on the planet of Tralfalmadore:

> *The alien zoo guide explained the primitive human's view of time this way: Imagine that you were looking across a desert at a mountain range on a day that was twinkling bright and clear. You could look at a peak or a bird or a cloud, at a stone right in front of you, or even down a canyon behind those things. But among them was this poor Earthling, and his head was encased in a steel sphere which he could never take off. There was only one eyehole through which he could look, and welded to that eyehole were six feet of pipe.*
>
> *This was only the beginning of the Earthling's miseries, because he was also strapped to a steel lattice which was bolted to a flatcar on rails, and there was no way he could turn his head or touch the pipe. The far end of the pipe rested on a bi-pod which was also bolted to the flatcar. All the Earthling could see was the little dot at the end of the pipe. He didn't know he was on a flatcar, didn't even know there was anything peculiar about his situation.*
>
> *The flatcar sometimes crept, sometimes went extremely fast, often stopped—went uphill, downhill, around curves, along straightaways. Whatever the poor earthling saw through the pipe, he had no choice but to say, "That's life."*

C.S. Lewis has a few more ideas for illustrating God's "eternal now" point of view:

Almost certainly God is not in Time. His life does not consist of moments following one another. If a million people are praying to him at 10:30 tonight, He need not listen to them all in that one little snippet which we call ten-thirty. Ten-thirty—and every other moment from the beginning of the world—is always the Present for him. If you like to put it that way, He has all eternity in which to listen to the split second of prayer put up by a pilot as his plane crashes in flames.

Suppose I am writing a novel. I write: "Mary laid down her work; next moment came a knock at the door." For Mary, who has to live in the imaginary time of my story, there is no interval between putting down the work and hearing the knock. But I, who am Mary's maker, do not live in that imaginary time at all. Between writing the first half of that sentence and the second, I might sit down for three hours and think steadily of Mary. I could think about Mary as if she were the only character in the book and for as long as I pleased, and the hours I spent in doing so would not appear in Mary's time (the time inside the story) at all.

God is not hurried along in the Time-stream of this universe any more than an author is hurried along in the imaginary time of his own novel. He has infinite attention to spare for each one of us. He does not have to deal with us in the mass. You are as much alone with Him as if you were the only being He had ever created.

With that thought in mind, I ponder the following lyric as if it were written from God to me:

If I could save time in a bottle
The first thing that I'd like to do
Is to save every day

Till Eternity passes away
Just to spend them with you

If I could make days last forever
If words could make wishes come true
I'd save every day like a treasure and then
Again, I would spend them with you
(Jim Croce, "Time in a Bottle," *Greatest Hits*, 1973)

Isn't it intriguing that the present... the now... is where we as human beings always are and exist within, and yet it is utterly impossible to define. The moment I say I am in the present, it has actually slipped immediately into the past, before the words—or even the thought—can be completed.

Yancey adds:

We experience time in a sequence—morning happens, then afternoon, then evening—but we do all our thinking in the present. If I think about the breakfast I ate earlier this morning, I think in the present about what happened in the past. If I contemplate dinner this evening, I think in the present about what will happen in the future. Because I only exist in the present, I can only perceive the past and the future from the perspective of the present.

We accelerate our days
To look into Your eyes
(Yes, "Sound Chaser," from *Relayer*, 1975)

That indefinable moment that is the border between the past and the future is what we inhabit; where we are; it is the essence of Life itself. Sometimes, don't you feel like you've gotten just a glimpse of eternity? A moment where all seems in harmony and you have a peaceful and joyous perspective that almost seems to make time stand still... or at least slow down? These moments are so profound—so moving to us—that they stay with us our entire lives. I think this deep knowing is "the eternal now." Since we are infinite souls encased in finite bodies, we yearn for it, yet we can't fully comprehend it in our current circumstance.

So when it comes to our relationship to "the eternal now," a lot of us have the idea that it's all been fixed before the very foundations of the earth. Once again; the answer would be *Yes* and *No.* Tony Campolo puts it this way:

> *Before the foundation of the earth, and this very moment with God, are exactly the same. So right now, if you make a decision, it is made not only now, but before history began—and throughout eternity. Every moment is fraught with eternal significance; every moment is an opportunity to make a decision that has eternal ramifications—that reaches back and reaches forward.*

> **Try to see yourself where you want to be**
> **Not in the place where you've dug**
> **Live for the moment, not yesterday**
> **Don't sit around and wait for someone to say**
> **Come on, let's go**
> **Live in the moment**
> **Don't wait for one**
> (Monte Montgomery, "Let's Go," from *Monte Montgomery,* 2008)

Campolo continues:

When I commit myself to the here and now, it is not as though I am dealing with an a priori meaning to my existence. It means that here and now I decide what the logical direction of my existence is. God does not decide without consulting with me on what I should do with my life. "Come now and let us reason together, saith the Lord" (Isaiah 1:18). He comes alongside each one of us and says, "Come on, let's talk, let's pray, let's relate, let's enter into dialogue." To be a Christian is to live in the context of an ongoing dialogue with God, and every moment of every day is a decision moment... a commitment moment. It's not as though you make one decision and that's that. There are endless arrays of commitments that must be made as we travel along life's road. It's never over. It's over and over and over again. For every moment of every day. I am in dialogue with Jesus. It's an ongoing conversation. We are deciding together; we work out together what I am going to do and who I am going to be; He does not decide without my consent.

There's a common theology I think most of us resent that goes something like this:

"God has a plan for your life."

And we ask: "Well what is it?"

And the response is: *"I don't know."*

"Well how do I find out?"

"Ummm, I don't know."

"Well, if God has a plan for my life and I don't live that way... If I go a different direction, then what happens?"

"Then you're living in sin."

Well, it just doesn't seem fair to me that there would be this plan that He doesn't tell me about, and then if I don't follow it, that He would be angry at my disobedience.

Campolo concludes:

The truth is that God is right here with us in every moment of every day: walking with us, talking with us, reasoning with us, Campolo concludes. That's why the Bible encourages us to pray constantly; that's why Jesus encouraged us to be in fellowship with him constantly. Prayer is not some little exercise we do on the side... Prayer is the ongoing decision process that happens moment-by-moment, day-by-day. We choose. In the present, we define who we are; God helps us interpret what we have been through, and we define the future together.

What a tremendous hope this brings! What an intriguing prospect that every moment of my life is meaningful in the here and now but also carries eternal ramifications. Henry Thoreau said, "You can't kill time without injuring eternity." I don't want to waste the Now that I am in. I want to make it count.

Wish the sun to stand still
Reaching out to touch our own being
Past all mortal as we
Here we can be
We can be here
Like the time I ran away
And turned around
And You were standing close to me
(Yes, "Awaken," from *Going For The One*, 1977)

CHAPTER 21

CHECKERS

I wonder what you'd think if all the changes didn't come
For growing old is only going back to where you're from
(Kansas, "Incomudro" from *Song For America*, 1974)

I have never defeated my Dad at checkers. I am officially zero for a lifetime against him. In my teens, I began to beat him at chess and still capture his king more than half the time when I play him now. As I progressed in my youth, I was able to start winning when I played him in ping pong, Monopoly, and croquet. As I matured, I was exultant when I realized I could hit baseballs farther, toss softballs harder, and throw a longer and tighter spiral football pass than he. And I could see the pride in his eyes when he realized he had taught me well.

But checkers... harrumph! I've never seen anyone so adept at thinking at least three moves ahead and setting up dastardly double, triple, and even *quadruple* jumps. And it's not like chess where you have choices... When a jump is set up for your move in checkers, you *have* to take it—which is how he'd set up his ambush for several volleys. And it wasn't just me... At family reunions and church gatherings, he would pretty much dismember anyone who tangled with him on the black and red board.

Last night, however; I beat him, and I was doing everything in my power *not* to.

Dad had a stroke two weeks ago. His health has been on a steady decline the past three years, ever since Mom passed away suddenly. Everyone—including Dad himself—always figured he would be the first to go, since he had battled prostate cancer sixteen years ago and had a triple bypass a decade back. But life has a way of shuffling the deck differently than we expect.

Love lost, such a cost
Give me things
that don't get lost
Like a coin that won't get tossed
Rolling home to you
I've been first and last
Look at how the time goes past
But I'm all alone at last
Rolling home to you

Old man take a look at my life
I'm a lot like you
I need someone to love me
the whole day through
Ah, one look in my eyes
and you can tell that's true
(Neil Young, "Old Man" from *Harvest*, 1972)

Less than a year after Mom's death, he felt that taking care of their suburban two-story home and large yard was beginning to drain him. He resolutely refused any idea of moving closer to either of us... He wanted to stay close to his extended family and church fellowship in the Allegheny hills. My sister Joyce and I helped him visit four retirement communities and all decided on a terrific complex in picturesque Zelienople, PA, about forty miles north of his neighborhood. We scaled down about two-thirds of his possessions, sold the house, and moved him into a cottage where he still had some autonomy. It was great for him to keep his beloved dog, Peppy, as well as be able to drive that lumbering Buick of his, cook his own meals, do his own laundry, etc.

Just eighteen months into his stay, it was becoming increasingly hard for him to maintain even at that level. He was becoming more and more forgetful. He nearly burned the place down one day when he melted a tea pot on the stove. We talked a lot with him and the administration of the retirement community and all agreed that the time was right to move into an "assisted living" apartment. So, once again, we had to sift out another half of his possessions in order to go from a nine-hundred-square-foot home to fifty-five-percent less in a two-room dwelling. He was thankfully still able to keep the pup and the car. But now he wouldn't need to worry about cooking, laundry, or being out in the elements quite as much... and the staff would come twice a day to help him with the seventeen-or-so medications he needed to take.

Now, just half a year later, even this has become overwhelming to him. He has fallen at least five times (several due to getting tangled up in Peppy's leash while taking him for "walkies"), but none with serious repercussions, thank goodness. He's also been getting more confused with his bookkeeping. This has always been a real source of pride for him, having graduated at the top of his class in accounting at Duquesne University. In my daily calls, I was hearing heightened levels of stress in his voice as tax time was approaching.

Both Joyce and I could see dramatic decline in his stature and color with each visit we would make. He has shrunk from five-foot-eleven to around five-foot-five in the last several years. His hair has turned white and his skin has become ever paler.

At the end of April, I got the call that Dad was wandering up and down the hallways of the retirement home: asking people if they would like to order ice cream and taking down copious numbers on a bizarre chart he was keeping. When the nurses asked if they could help him, he began speaking strictly in numbers. They called me, and we all concluded that something was definitely amiss. He was rushed to the hospital... but since it was a Friday night, the results of the tests weren't going to be conclusive until they were analyzed the following week.

I spoke with Dad several times each day, and he was still mixing in lots of numerical jargon into his answers. Sometimes with strokes, the wires get crossed in the brain, and folks will defer back to things they are very comfortable with, like a long-forgotten foreign language from their youth. Joyce and I would try to chat normally with him and act as if the mathematical answers to our questions were normal... but it was more than a little disturbing.

Sail away, away
Ripples never come back
They've gone to the other side
Look into the pool
Ripples never come back
Dive to the bottom and go to the top
To see where they have gone
Oh, they've gone to the other side...
(Genesis, "Ripples" from *A Trick of the Tail*, 1976)

As expected, when the test results were deciphered, it was indeed a stroke. And it has apparently taken a lot out of Pop. His strength is now so diminished that he has to use a wheel chair most of the time. Fortunately, the arithmetic in his speech has gone away, but about half the time, he's in deep water as he toils to finish any cogent thoughts. He seems better in the morning, but as the day progresses, he loses steam.

While I was with him last week, I could see him strain tremendously trying to formulate and express answers to fairly simple questions. He would furrow his brow, look off in the distance and try to focus... but after getting a few words out, he'd usually just trail off and then start shaking his head in pained frustration.

His sense of humor seemed intact, though, and he laughed often at little comments others and I would make. His big, toothy smile was still present much of the time. A few days ago, he was wearing his custom-made "Doggie Doodle" t-shirt I had given him a few Christmases ago. On the back, it says: "Ask me to tell you one of my dog jokes." Dad has a million of 'em. So I asked him if he had a good one for me that morning. He smiled and said, "Why sure..." An awkward pause ensued; he lifted his right hand and pointed as if to some catalogue of one liners just hanging there... desperately wanting to pull one out to share... but he just couldn't. He lowered his head, nearly in shame, and sighed deeply.

The writer stares with glassy eyes
Defies the empty page
His beard is white, his face is lined
And streaked with tears of rage

Thirty years ago, how the words would flow
With passion and precision

But now his mind is dark and dulled
By sickness and indecision

And he stares out the kitchen door
Where the sun will rise no more
(Rush, "Losing It" from *Signals*, 1982)

We went out for several walks on the grounds. It is a lovely community, and they have nice walking paths that are smooth for wheelchairs, too. He enjoyed looking at all the huge goldfish in one of the ponds. He wanted to stick his hand under the cascading water of a fountain. I pulled him under a blooming cherry tree so he could pull down a branch and breath in the perfumed blossoms.

After more meetings with the staff, it has become apparent that Dad will most likely never be able to return to his apartment. He will be in full nursing care from here on out. Of course, this means no more driving, no more personal accounting/freedom of finances, and sadly, no more Peppy. We found a good family with children for the dog (they will bring him by for visits), began the process of selling his car, and are taking over all his mail, billing, taxes, etc. On one hand, I can tell this vexes him, but on the other, I can sense he's relieved. And we will need to condense his belongings yet again. How hard it is to discard a lifetime of memories on such short order.

After dinner last night, I thought that perhaps playing a game of checkers would help his confidence. What is normally about a fifteen-minute exercise in humility for me turned into nearly an hour of torment for both of us. The wheels were turning as he examined the board, but he was unable to think ahead. I was doing everything possible to arrange for set-ups where he could jump me, but he seemed to choose other options at each chance. And he walked right into some jumps that I had to take. It pained me each time.

In at least twenty instances, I had to remind Dad that it was in-deed his turn, and I'd have to show him again what move I had just made. He would keep totaling up the pieces that remained, shake his head and utter, "Holy Smokies." I can't ever recall him saying that phrase before... but he must've said it a dozen times during that game.

There is no pain, you are receding
A distant ships smoke on the horizon
You are only coming through in waves
Your lips move but I can't hear what you're sayin'
When I was a child I caught a fleeting glimpse
Out of the corner of my eye
I turned to look but it was gone
I cannot put my finger on it now
The child is grown, the dream is gone
I have become comfortably numb
(Pink Floyd, "Comfortably Numb" from *The Wall*, 1979)

As he struggled to hone in on the checkerboard, tears kept welling up in my eyes. He happened to glance up at me once, saw my condition and asked what was wrong. I deflected with: "Ah, it's these stupid allergies." And he nodded, knowing all-too-well the pollen wars that I inherited from him, especially each spring. I'd blow my nose and wipe my lids, but it was hard to watch what was unfolding before me.

Eventually, when he had no moves left to make that wouldn't result in tremendous losses, I looked at him and said, "How 'bout we call this one a draw?" He smiled meekly and said, "Awww, you beat me every which way here... Good game, Mark."

Victory never felt so hollow. Here's hoping he can beat the pants off me again soon.

> *It's better to burn out*
> *than it is to rust*
> *The king is gone*
> *but he's not forgotten*

(Neil Young, "Out of the Blue" from *Rust Never Sleeps*, 1979)

CHAPTER 22

COLD CUTS AND KNIFING WINDS

I arrived in Colorado Springs this afternoon for a few days of meetings and timed it to land just hours before a nasty winter storm. Oh, joy. It's snowing hard and blowing even harder. At dinnertime, the radio said the wind chill was down to negative twenty-two and dropping. It's got me recollecting a similar night when I lived here years ago...

One late December evening, after nineteen inches of snow had been dumped in just ten hours time, I was having dinner with some friends at a local eatery. We were talking about living one's faith out radically... making a difference not only with the larger sweeping motions of our lives, like how we vote, what we do for a living, how we invest our money... but also how we treat the waitress, what we do with that forty-five minutes we have "to kill" while waiting for an appointment, and who/what we think to remember in our supplications.

It was stimulating. A definite case of iron sharpening iron. I left there with an acute sense that I was going to make things count for more. No, I didn't have any Pollyannaish delusions of a master plan. I just wanted to be focused more on the here and now... take things a moment at a time, maybe even a day at a time at most... and see what might happen.

No more than half a mile from the restaurant on my way home, I noticed a guy stumbling as he was trying to make his way along the three-foot snow banks that lined the street. And for some reason, he didn't have coat on. As was often the case after a Front Range blizzard, the clouds passed, the high skies followed, and without any low atmospheric insulation, what little warmth there was was pulled high into the air. It was colder than a well diggers butt. Maybe ten degrees—and the wind was blowing, dropping the skin temp to well below zero.

My initial thought was that he was scurrying along to someone's home nearby; why else would someone venture out without sufficient covering? But I sensed the Spirit telling me to stop, back up, and see if this guy needed a lift somewhere.

As I reversed my track, I saw from the rear view mirror that he began to slip awkwardly, almost as if he were trying to get away. He lost his balance and fell heavily into a drift. I got out and said, "Do you need some help... Do you need a ride?"

He looked up and realized I was a stranger. Apparently he had initially been worried otherwise. Picking himself up sluggishly, he said, "Uh... yeah."

I made sure he could get to his feet alright and opened the passenger door for him. Once I got in and began driving, it became apparent that he had been in a fight—as some blood was draining out of his left ear. His shirt was torn with a few buttons missing. Even though he was covered with snow from his tumble, he didn't seem phased by the cold. Due to my car being like the inside of a freezer, the steam from his exhales gave away the liquor on his breath.

"Hi... I'm Mark," I began, hoping for some response. Nothing at first. "It's wicked out there tonight. Can I help you get somewhere?"

Finally, after a long pause from sizing me up, he mumbled, "Yeah. Timberview Apartments."

"I think I know where that is, but you'll need to guide me in to make sure." Another cavernous pause. "I noticed your cut—should we get that cleaned..."

Before I could finish, he cut me off with a harsh, "NO! I don't need any Good Samaritan. I just fought with a sonofabitch back there at that joint, and I think he's gonna come after me. I cut him. I just need to get to my place, get my stuff, and get the hell outta here."

Lots of things run through one's mind in a situation like this. I thought, *Am I in some danger with this guy? Will I be arrested as an accomplice in this? Is he crazed—Will he pull something on me?* It was after midnight; the streets were deserted. It was kind of a dicey scenario. I decided to just play it out... see where it would go. This was long before the wristbands came into vogue, but I pondered, *What would Jesus do?*

My passenger guided me to the complex, and we pulled up to his building. He realized he had left his keys in his coat back at the bar, but he "sure as shit wasn't going back there." His roommate was out of town for the holidays, so he thought he might be able to climb the gutter to the second story balcony and enter that way. It was so icy and windswept that he couldn't manage it, even with me trying to give him some boosts and him climbing on top of my shoulders at one point.

I realized he had nowhere to go. It was obvious he was afraid to call the police or a hospital because of the confrontation at the bar. From previous experience helping other folks, I knew that the homeless shelter wouldn't allow people to enter after 9 PM. Emboldened by my earlier conversation at the restaurant, I asked him if he'd like to stay at my place for the night.

"You don't know me from Satan," he said. An unsettling response to be sure.

"Well, all I know is you don't have any other options right now, and I'm extending an invitation. Nothing fancy—I got a couch in front of a fireplace you can use."

As he surmised his circumstance, he hesitantly said, "OK... sure."

I reintroduced myself. This time he reciprocated by telling me his name was Johnny. We got to talking as we made our way north on Academy Boulevard, the snow-packed roadway crunching loudly under my frozen tires. He was originally from Pennsylvania and had worked his way out west during the past few years, bouncing from one job to the next. Since I was from PA myself, we were able to establish some camaraderie around towns, geography, and sports teams.

By the time we made it to my apartment twenty minutes later, he had softened up... even laughing a few times. The car was getting toasty now, and his demeanor had warmed considerably, too.

When we got in, I made up some hot coffee and cocoa; I opened my first-aid kit so he could apply some creams, gauze, etc. to his wounds, got him set up so he could take a shower, and gave him some clothes he could wear while we washed his others. As he cleaned up, I prepared a makeshift bed for him on the couch and got some logs out to start a blaze in the fireplace.

While he was drying his hair, I noticed he was sobering up a bit. I told him to make himself at home: that since it was a Friday night, I wasn't in a hurry to wake up in the morning but would be glad to take him back down to his apartment if he wanted to get in with a pass key from the front office. He admitted that he was staying there as a guest and that the management wouldn't know him; he wasn't sure they would help him out.

"Let's figure it out tomorrow. Get some rest in the meantime," I told him.

Maybe I'm just too trusting a soul. Perhaps I was feeling euphoric about helping someone who was truly in need. But more than anything, I was just curious to see where God was going to lead with this. It would be dishonest to say I slept like a baby that night. I was just a *tad* concerned that I might wake up to find half my belongings gone, including my car. But I was determined not to make this guy feel judged or under intense scrutiny. I also didn't want to doubt that God was going to use this to teach me something.

The next morning, I awoke to some music coming from my stereo in the living room. Johnny had picked out a Robin Trower album and was jamming to the slowhand psychedelic blues.

I whipped up some eggs, bacon, toast, and oatmeal. We wolfed it down, and Johnny began to open up. He told me some about his upbringing: where he'd gone to school, what types of jobs he'd had. Then he asked me why I had done what I did.

Figuring I had nothing to lose in telling the truth, I said that I did it because I felt it was what Jesus would do and that maybe I could learn something valuable from it all. I told him I had taken some homeless people in before but never anyone who might be "on the run from the law."

"You know, I figured it might be something like that," he said, as he surveyed my little apartment. "I saw some of your religious books here this morning before you woke up. I noticed some of the Christian rock albums in your collection, along with the Mahoghany Rush, Tom Waits, Judas Priest, and U2—Man, you got some weird-ass taste. But I like it."

Then he did something I'll long remember. He quickly turned around and dug something out of his pile of dirty clothes: He spun back toward me and flicked open a switchblade, waving it within a few feet of my face. "Ya know, I coulda cut you last night, too. I coulda robbed you blind. You're a sucker to believe that Jesus shit. It ain't gonna do you no good in the long run."

Keeping a calm exterior, I summoned up as much peace as I could, while simultaneously being buzzed with adrenaline. "Well, why didn't you?" I asked, staring straight into his pupils.

With that, he lowered his knife. He took a long, deep, sorrowful sigh and began looking away from me. I saw his eyes start to well up. Johnny started to say something but began to stammer. I knew better than to say anything... *Just let him vent*, I thought.

After several long, sniffling breaths, he began to relay how he had been in the Teen Challenge drug rehab program, run by Christians in eastern Pennsylvania, several years before. A rather forward-thinking judge in Philadelphia had given him the option of either going through T.C. or going to jail. Johnny had gotten clean and sober, and he was just a few weeks from graduating when he decided to split. He had been in and out of trouble across the continent since then. A Bible and a couple other books the program had given him were still in his possession... but he just wasn't sure he really wanted to battle his demons. "Maybe God has given up on me. I sure know that I have," he confessed.

I'm not one to pontificate with lots of platitudes... I don't have a clue much of the time as to what to do—let alone say—in a given situation. I took a deep breath of my own and simply said, "Well, I don't think Jesus gives up on any of us. If there's anything I can do to help you find the way, I'll do it."

"Why should you give a rat's ass about me?" he whispered.

"I'm really not sure... I just know that I'm supposed to offer help. Besides, I don't think you're as far away as you think. I think he's here all the time just waiting for us to surrender."

Johnny stayed with me for several days. There were a few other moments where he acted schizoid, and I thought he might snap and do something weird. But I felt a kind of strange peace overriding my apprehensions. We had several long talks about God and about scripture, but mostly we talked about Jesus. We prayed a couple of times. Honest, no-frills, gutsy prayers. Eventually we found his roommate, and Johnny said he was going to try and get things worked out and even to attempt to make things right with the confrontation he'd had at that lounge.

I spoke with him a couple more times over the next month. He sounded like he was getting back on the right track. "I think God wants me to head back to Pennsylvania to finish out the program and finally get this substance abuse behind me," he declared.

Another week passed, and I called his number, but it was disconnected. I never heard from Johnny again.

There's no dramatic sense of closure to this story. However; what I learned over that long weekend will resonate with me, I believe, for the rest of MY life. If I make myself available, all sorts of redemptive stuff can happen for me as well as those I come in touch with. There have been other homeless guys I've taken in. There have been more hitch hikers. Divine appointments with unclear conclusions. Strange winds sometimes blow intriguing persons into and then out of our lives.

Why did that happen? Perhaps the doing of the thing is often more important than its initial perceived "meaning." I guess it's that hope of things not seen. It's aiming out past what is promised, anticipating what good may be even beyond that.

I'm looking forward to learning the end of Johnny's story someday. It helps warm me on cold nights like these.

CHAPTER 23

SLEEPING WITH MARC WOZNIAK

I met Marc Wozniak in the summer of '82, not long after I had moved to Smashville. I had just become Petra's manager, working out of a temporary office in the dining room of lead singer Greg X. Volz. "Woz" had been working the better part of the year as the band's sole roadie. Since they were on the road nearly non-stop, he kept no permanent residence—opting to live in the Volz's back driveway in a bludgeoned, pea-green late-60s Chevy van that had been painted with a brush. Then—as now—Marc was dedicated, focused, and willing to pitch in wherever a need existed. He liked poetry, science fiction, progressive rock, *The Life of Brian*, and debate. We became friends in short order.

Let me state for the record that I am not homophobic, nor do I think that I have some deep-seeded homoerotic tendencies. But, Woz and I have shared a bed on more than one occasion.

The first time was on the fifty-two-day road trip that opened the *More Power To Ya Tour*, which later became known as the "Kill the Band Tour." Forty-four shows in a little under two months from coast to coast, border to border: covering twenty-four states and over 8,000 miles. In those days, the group traveled in a box van with a ten-foot trailer, and rooming was usually an adventure. Often staying in people's homes (dealing with pee-stained children's sheets, cat hair covered pillows, nine people using one bathroom without enough hot water, unexplained odors, obstacle course filled rooms—you get the picture), or campus guest housing at colleges (creaky bunk beds and the joys of showering with dozens of strangers), or lodging in non-electrified cabins in campgrounds (cold and clammy, with an assortment of insects that would keep even the most rabid entomologist jumpy). And those were the nights of concerts. On travel days—when no promoter was responsible for supplying lodging—we had to utilize what little money was allocated in the budget to put eight people in two or three fleabag motel rooms.

One such night, while I was out on the road with the band for a few days, we were at some ramshackle motor inn in northern Indiana. It was October, and temperatures were already below freezing. The band's Mark Kelly and John Slick were sharing a room with Woz and me, using two sagging, sunken twin size beds. The décor was "early trailapark" and the room stank of Pine-Sol and wet cigarettes. The thermostat was busted, but instead of being too chilly, it was the reverse—it was hotter than Beelzebub's armpit.

I discovered that night that Marc is a somewhat restless sleeper—he's got the jimmy-leg going at times. He tosses, turns, and mumbles. Combine that with the stuffy air, and I was in claustrophobic Hades the entire evening. It was so warm that I had to go sit outside at certain stretches so as not to suffocate. Not being able to sleep, I intermittently sat on a chair or tried stretching out on top of the covers. Woz was such a hard worker that it was no problem for him to "saw logs" in the most adverse conditions. No wonder, because I would daily see him lift 200-pound cabinets, pack the entire truck in twenty-five minutes, and tenaciously traverse ridiculous load-ins up stairwells and meandering hallways.

I watched admiringly as he would unwind and then recharge after several hectic eighteen-hour days in succession. As the years have passed, I learned from him that when you are tired enough, you can sleep ANYwhere, under ANY circumstance.

The second sequence of sleeping together happened a few years later. Petra had become much more successful, selling millions of albums and regularly packing-out major arenas. Woz was joined by over a dozen other crewmembers, and he now had the more "official" title of Stage Manager. But he still worked his butt off, even nearly getting killed once when he was electrocuted with faulty wiring during a power distribution tie-in. Witnesses said the blue arc that went from the box to his body shot him ten feet backwards. His coif looked like Buckwheat's, and the hair on his arms and eyebrows had been singed off. He was woozy for days. Due to the band's hectic road pace—and his responsibilities to repair equipment whenever they were off the road—Marc still hadn't really settled into any regular habitat while they were home in Tennessee.

On the early summer leg of the *Beat the System Tour*, a strange illness started to befall him. Open sores began forming on his neck, shoulders, and back. Woz was noticeably weakened, and the skin lesions began stinging. After several days, he finally succumbed to seeing a doctor, who declared that he had shingles... an odd ailment where long-dormant cells left-over from childhood chicken pox somehow regenerate, and a much more intense outbreak occurs. No one knows exactly why or when it will happen. One thing is for sure, however; physical labor is pretty much out of the question.

The band sent him home to Nashville, but the family that had been letting him use their spare bedroom decided, essentially, that he was "unclean." They didn't want him staying there with such an illness. He called some other friends, but they were unwilling.

When he came into the management office the day after arriving, he looked terrible from the sickness, but also from lack of sleep—turns out he had spent the night in his old van again.

When I heard this, I said, "You're staying with me." I shared a three-bedroom apartment with two other guys. They weren't fond of the idea of him sleeping on the couch with that kind of oozing rash, so I let him sleep in my bed. The couch wouldn't work for me, since it was short, with hard wooden armrests at each end, making it nearly impossible to accommodate a long build. So, I joined him in my king size.

Shingles is non-contagious, but it still carries a great stigma among many. It looks nasty, and the sharp pain from each scab can rage for hours at a stretch. It is most likely the disease that was described as "boils covering the skin" of Job. But Woz was my friend, and there was no need for him to suffer any more than he had to. Besides, we had some great conversations each evening as we were trying to drift off to sleep. I learned a lot about patience and long-suffering from Marc as I watched him deal with that pain. And I was reminded of those lessons years later when a much smaller bout of shingles struck me in 2004.

The third shared-bed story is the strangest. Another year had passed, and Woz had just gotten married. It was Christmastime, and he and his bride, Caroline, thought it would be fun to have some close friends who were stranded in Nashville for the holiday spend it at their home. We had a festive feast on the eve, including some dancing, board games, and charades... all of it punctuated with loads of laughs. Rather than having mixed singles sleeping together, we devised a plan where guys would room with guys, gals with gals, and all would be well with the world for one night. Since we had shared a boudoir before, Woz and I ended up in his waterbed.

As with the other scenarios, Marc was still an active sleeper: his movements accented all the more by the undulating waves of the aqua mattress. Midway through the night in his deep slumber—no doubt being accustomed to his wedded bliss—he rolled over and "spooned" me. I'm a fairly light sleeper, and, needless to say, this definitely caught my attention. I moved my hips and shoulders away from his torso a few inches, thinking he would get the message. He rolled a bit onto his back and mumbled something in his sleep.

Just as I was starting to doze off again, he turned back into me, then flung his arm over my shoulder and began to nuzzle my neck. I lay on my side utterly petrified. Taking a quick inventory of the situation, I sized-up my options. *Perhaps*, I pondered to myself, *He will come to his senses momentarily*. I tried to move farther from him, nearly hanging over the edge of the bed. In his stupor, he snuggled even closer.

Fearing that "little Woz" might soon make an appearance, I was, to say the least, no longer drowsy. My eyes were open wider than Goldie Hawn's on crack-cocaine. I couldn't help but nervously grin, as this was becoming surreal. I nudged Marc with my elbow, trying to give him a further non-verbal message. This only seemed to encourage this Casanova in his dream-state, as he murmured adoringly, "Caroline"...*long, dreamy breath*... "Ohhh, Caroline."

Dreading what embarrassment might ensue, I decided—in the words of Barney Fife—to "Nip it in the bud!" I once again, with even more force, elbowed his ribs. He kind of chuckled in his unconscious state, thinking that Caroline might be "playing hard to get." Then I gave him another shot and said, "Woz! It's me, Hollingsworth!"

There was a pregnant pause, and then as he came to his senses, this blushing "Ohhhhh, nooooo" realization as he rolled onto his back. "Ohh, maaaan..." (a few more deep breaths/sighs and then...) "Well..._This_ is embarrassing."

We both started to chuckle... then began to shake as we tried to contain what should've been torrents of laughter—we didn't want to wake up the rest of the household. To this day, it will come up in odd reminiscings between us and other friends, always accompanied with hysterics that we had to suppress on that eve. That night has become known as "Feely's Navidad." *Planes, Trains, and Automobiles* didn't hit the theaters for two more years, but I don't think the infamous: "Those aren't PILLOWS!" scene was any funnier.

So whether in an overheated hotel room, or sharing a sick bed, or fighting off his misplaced trance-like advances in his newlywed state, I've not only survived but have loved sleeping with Marc Wozniak.

PART THREE

WHAT IS AND
WHAT SHOULD BE

CHAPTER 24

THE WHY IN WYOMING

I am now, finally, in my fiftieth state: Wyoming. Odd that it took me so long to get here, since I lived just to the south in Colorado for six years in the late '80s. Always meant to make the short drive... but always put it off for one reason or another. What an idiot.

This trip comes at a time when I need to identify some questions that are formulating within me... and maybe even explore some answers. Both tend to happen best when I'm alone.

For the past two days, I've been skimming across the slightly rolling expanses of prairie stubble. There is a hallowed majesty to this far-flung sweep—reminiscent of traversing Alligator Alley in south Florida across the stark Everglades... the hellacious flats of Death Valley... the towering cornfield canyons and soybean savannahs of Illinois... the desolate Kansas-like grasslands of interior Turkey... the glacier-scraped moraines of Wisconsin... the untouched Serengeti of Kenya stretching into Tanzania... the high sierra plains of eastern Washington... the vast wheat lands of Alberta... the dead air-baked earth of south Mississippi... the marshy tracts of Alaska's Kenai Peninsula... the Bolivian Altiplano stretching eastward off the backside of the Andes... and the unending prickly sage spread across west Texas, New Mexico, and Arizona. It's intimidating, yet somehow sanctified.

Grasses are bent flat from steady mariahs. Sparrows struggle to fly sideways against these relentless gales. A random slice of plastic sheeting is caught and tethered against its will on a barbed wire, whipping frenetically, yearning for release. Cottonwoods hunker down in a small creek bed: each one deformed and gnarled from fighting the prevailing westerlies and winter's incalculable wrath. Tumbleweeds—some the circumference of a baby pool—meander across the roadway, pushed to who-knows-where by the unseen and unyielding force. I sit on a small butte and let the godly gusts envelope me; speak to me …

When I'm needing a friend I can talk to the wind
God I sure am glad that I found him
Sometimes he seems to be the only one beside me
Who can feel the Lord's breath all around him
Winter's cold frozen ice or a bright autumn day
On a warm summer night you can hear him say

Cry for me, sigh for me, sad my breezes flow
Stay for me, play for me, the song my friends will know
My lonely wind must blow
(Kansas, "Lonely Wind" from *Kansas*, 1974)

While hurtling across the imposing fields in my car, at a speed we can only dream of in city life, a mama elk and her calf bound across the highway just in front of me. As the day progresses, I later encounter one, two, even three rotting carcasses of albino caribou that were not as quick in their evasion. A skinny rabbit—or was it the mythological jackalope (I thought I saw a glint of antlers?)—darts in front of me, narrowly missing a sudden demise.

What little land is agriculturally developed primarily yields hay. SUV-sized harvested rolls dot the slight hillsides as if it were Paul Bunyan's shredded wheat. On the straightaways, vehicles that are two miles ahead of me shimmer from the heat rising off the blacktop. I race a Union Pacific train with 113 cars of coal, so heavily laden that there are two locomotives pushing from behind as well as two in the lead.

I pass through the town of Kreeline, which from all I can gather is made up of a cinder block home, a double-wide trailer, and the Three Sisters Truck Stop Café. I am equal parts amused and awe-struck at other outposts I survey, like Chugwater, Fort Hat Creek, Roberts Roost, Buffalo Jump, Aladdin, Egbert, Guernsey, Van Tassell, Jay Em, Beulah, and Sundance—where I write this tonight. I wonder if I would have had the tenacity and courage to explore and live off these wastelands, like the Native Americans did for thousands of years and the pioneers who came later.

I wonder if I truly have the desire to explore deep inside the broad expanse of my soul to find why I am so restless and lonely now.

Yesterday I saw mile-upon-mile of twelve-foot high slatted snow fences, constructed to help divert deep drifting across these lifeline highways during blizzards. Having been through enough Midwestern winters to know, these attempts to stem the tide of nature are somewhat humorous. I suppose they can fool themselves into thinking they're making a difference—and perhaps occasionally they do. I shake my head, thinking that I often do the same with temporary diversions in my mind. But I know that ultimately, it is only the thawing power of God's forgiveness that can disintegrate these obstructions that I sometimes build up with time, and in other instances, that I allow to hastily overtake me.

On one hand, you have to admire the dedication needed to dig and string the plethora of fence posts criss-crossing these plains. But on the other; it's nearly laughable to think that land this imposing, this spacious, this illimitable... can really be cordoned off and contained. I usually look at God that way. I am sometimes haughty enough to think I can control what, more often than not, is unpredictable and unwilling to be tamed.

> *Mighty friend that is mine, can you show me a sign?*
> *He'll leave nothing but only to hear him*
> *I've seen the tall trees bend low when the mighty winds blow*
> *And that's all the more reason I fear him*
> *Hear him call for the earth's lonely, I can feel his great pain*
> *But on the eve of this day*
> *I'll join in his refrain*
>
> *Cry for me, sigh for me, sad my breezes flow*
> *Stay for me, play for me, the song my friends will know*
> *My lonely wind must blow*
> (Kansas, "Lonely Wind" from *Kansas*, 1974)

Sandstone bluffs and escarpments rise and fall periodically along my journey through this far-flung expanse. The Chinooks have worn them down over the eons, revealing layers of long-forgotten oceans now exposed to the cutting atmosphere. What epochs' worth of hidden secrets in bone and fossil are yet to be revealed?

Am I willing to be peeled back? Laid open? Exposed? Will I be surprised at what lies beneath my time-tested surface?

This afternoon, I passed a huge ranch where I saw one big Black

Angus bull—all by his lonesome—staring longingly through a fence toward the highway and beyond. No other cattle within miles.

Why is that image haunting me?

Perhaps someday I'll experience the enormous Outback Down Under, the Steppes of Uzbekistan, the measureless sands of the Sahara... see the long-legged foxes of the Patagonian Plateau in Argentina, the wild steeds of the Mongolian Desert, and Canada's untamed Nunavut northern territories. But for now, the mammoth sweep of Wyoming is intimidating enough, both externally and to my interior.

On a knoll off a two-lane road between Orin and Lusk, a lone cross constructed of railroad ties overlooks a twenty-mile-wide valley. It is hammered deep into the ground. Sure. Steadfast. Vigilant.

When I'm needing a friend, I'll remember the wind
And my life here with the breezes of sorrow
I'll be leaving him soon 'cause I've got to make room
For the lonely who will find him tomorrow
On a black stormy night in your bosom I'll cling
And I'll know I've found love and this last song we'll sing

Cry for me, sigh for me, sad my breezes flow
Stay for me, play for me, the song my friends will know
My lonely wind... my lonely wind... my lonely wind must blow.
(Kansas, "Lonely Wind" from *Kansas*, 1974)

CHAPTER 25

TI CHAPE

After passing by the hazed eastern tip of Cuba, our American Airlines flight banked steeply to the right, and within minutes we were passing over the northern peninsula of Haiti, so recognizable due to the heavily rutted landscape. The French had not been kind when they ravaged the once lush western half of Hispaniola of all the mahogany trees and shipped the lumber back to Paris to make fine furniture. Over two hundred years later, the nation is still ninety-percent barren, and what little good topsoil remains is being eroded into the Caribbean. We circled over the Canal du Sud Strait, approaching Port-au–Prince: a teeming city I had not been to in nineteen years. As we touched down on the single-runway "international" airport, memories began to take focus.

I had been to this "second poorest country in the world" three times in the '80s. In fact, my very first trip to a developing nation had been here in early 1984 when I was managing Petra. We had begun a relationship with Compassion a year earlier and had seen thousands of needy kids find sponsors via their enthusiastic concert audiences and album inserts. It was so humbling for us to meet some of the children we had been sponsoring and to see the life-changing results that child development in a Christian environment could bring about.

A wiry American with a unique accent was our guide on that trip. He had been living in Haiti for six years, assisting with various ministries and eventually signing on full-time with Compassion. His deep, expressive voice carried the influence of being raised as a missionary's son in West Africa, of having attended various universities in America earning multiple degrees, and of service as a linguist in the army on the Eastern Front of Europe. Along the way, he had mastered seven different languages, and we heard him speak fluently and persuasively in the unique language of Haiti known as Creole. Thus began a twenty-five-year friendship with the man who is now my boss. Wess Stafford has since gone on to become the president of Compassion International, overseeing the organization as it grew to twenty times the size it was then—now giving manifold assistance to over one million children in twenty-five countries.

I'll never forget when we were sitting in some sort of traffic back up—a very common Haitian occurrence—along the N1 Highway near the coastal town of Arcahaie. I snapped one of my all-time favorite photos: a little boy of about three with a distended belly from malnutrition, wearing a ragged striped t-shirt and nothing else, proudly hoisting his torn little hand-made kite on a ten-foot string made of whatever scraps of twine and wire he had found. The breeze was keeping it only about five feet aloft, but he was as gleeful as any child I had ever seen.

Wess was seated next to me in our van and noticed my fascination with the tiny urchin. "Ah, yes... another little Ti Chape," he observed.

"What is a Ti Chape?" I asked.

"It's a Creole phrase that many parents in these poorest areas of

Haiti use with their youngest kids," Wess explained. "I'm sure you'll hear it often over the next several days as we visit homes. It's a term of endearment... but it's also one of a harsh reality that reminds everyone, every time it is uttered, of how devastating each day can be for people living on the brink. Ti Chape means 'little survivor' or 'one who has escaped death.'"

By this time, several others from the band were leaning in close to hear what he was explaining.

As a very tenderhearted man, Wess could not conceal his passion for these people, and tears began to well in his eyes. With a catch in his throat, he continued: "Sadly, for the majority of the poor here in Haiti, the infant mortality rate is as high as fifty percent for children under the age of five. So often times, parents won't refer to their littlest ones by their birth name until they celebrate their fifth birthday, because they know all too well that many of them won't make it that far. While they are still in this most vulnerable toddler stage, they are affectionately called 'Ti Chape.' I guess it is overly painful to consistently call them by their real name in fear of assigning too much hope to their prospects. This same phenomena happens—by different names of course—in other desperately poor cultures around the globe."

I watched intently for a few more minutes at that toddler joyfully trying to keep his tattered toy buoyant on the air. Then we lurched forward in the traffic flow. For the rest of our stay, I pondered what his chances were really going to be within the next few months.

Later that day, I saw my first human corpse abandoned in one of the filthy alleyways of an intense slum on the bay known as City du la Sole. It wasn't the only one I would ever see in Haiti. Even now, whenever I look at the photo of the kite-toting lad in my collection, it gives me great pause, and it was all coming back to me twenty-five years later as we drove through the packed streets of Port au Prince.

On our final day of this just-completed trip, we drove out the N2 highway along the southern Massif de la Hotte peninsula, weaving past colorfully painted tap-taps (old pickups converted into buses often over-loaded with upwards of twenty people), soot-spewing diesel trucks, and UN troop patrol vehicles that help keep the peace in this politically unstable environment.

As we passed tiny farms, my mind drifted back to meeting Horele Georges. He was the third son of a meager dirt farmer near the town of Miragoane. Hector Georges supported his family of seven on a rocky plot about one-half an acre in size. He toiled with his single emaciated cow nearly every daylight hour, trying to squeeze each ounce of productivity out of that parched earth as was humanly possible.

When Horele was registered into the program at age five, he began learning new agricultural techniques that showed how yield could be increased dramatically with the help of better seeds, certain fertilizers, irrigation techniques, and so on.

A year passed as he observed through a couple of growth seasons how the corn at the project was markedly bigger than what was growing on all the area farms. Horele started asking Hector if they could try these processes on their crops. At first, his father just ignored him, but Horele persisted. Eventually Hector said, "Son, I've worked this land in this way my entire life. My father before me did the same, and your grandfather and great grandfather before them. There's nothing that can be done that we haven't tried."

But Horele knew that some of these ideas had not been put into practice—or at least he wasn't aware that they had been—while he helped his father every day before and after school. So he continued trying to explain to his poppa what he had been taught. As it was just the beginning of a new planting season, Hector finally relented and said, "Alright, Horele. I'll let you have one row of this section where you can try your silly tricks. I'll be surprised if whatever it is you try even survives the first heat wave."

Taking what he had learned at the Compassion project, the little boy eagerly set his attention on that modest row of newly planted seeds. Each morning, he tilled and watered. Each afternoon, he blended in the fertilizing techniques he was being taught, pulled weeds, and watered more.

Eight weeks passed, and lo and behold, Horele's row was two feet taller than the rest of the plot. His daddy had certainly noticed but kept waiting for the stalks to wither. When it was apparent that his little son's crop was indeed going to be substantially better than his, he sheepishly said, "So, son,... ummm...What is it exactly that they are teaching you to do?"

By the time the next growing season was finished, Hector Georges' little farm was producing a forty-percent higher yield than it ever had.

I look back fondly on Horele, because he was a boy I sponsored for twelve years. And I finally met him less than four months before he was to graduate from high school, near the top of his class. His dad became so good at the farming techniques his little son had taught him, that he became a regular volunteer assistant with each new class at the Compassion project. Skepticism—and even fatalism—had been superseded by the youthful zeal of his child. Hector eventually ended up on staff at the project.

Horele is in his mid-thirties now, with a family of his own. He's a leader in his church and in his community. And on the same tiny scrap of land, he's still raising some of the best corn on that side of the island.

It was easy to assess that not much had changed for the better in Haiti since that visit in 1990. There were still massive piles of stinking refuse at nearly every street corner. Sewers were packed and overflowing with debris. The charcoal-based energy and cooking lifestyle was still causing a thick haze that covered most urban areas. And tens of thousands of people packed every sidewalk and spilled out into the bumpy streets… just barely avoiding dismemberment from crazed motorists.

We were headed out to see one of Compassion's projects that had been in existence for twenty-three years but had added a new program just a few years earlier that would help revolutionize our work.

We arrived in the rural town of Papette, where the Wesleyan Church had become a real community center over the past two decades, and it was obvious that the 1,000 residents had a deep respect for all that the Compassion project had helped them with over the years.

My little group of radio professionals and I were ushered into the sanctuary where ninety-three mothers and their infants had been patiently waiting. It was amazing how quiet and disciplined the 120-or-so little ones were; we commented amongst ourselves that the same scene in America would've been utter pandemonium. There was a look of gentle appreciation on the face of each young woman when we made eye contact.

A handful of the moms came forward to give testimony to what had revolutionized their lives. You see, over Compassion's fifty-six years of existence at that point, we'd always been laser-beam focused on child development for kindergarten-aged kids through high school. But five years prior, we had launched a new initiative called the Child Survival Program (CSP), which supports mothers and children all the way from their pregnancy, on into infancy, and through the toddler years.

One of the young mothers, Irmice, had her little eighteen-month-old boy draped over her shoulder, fast asleep, as she stood at the podium and shared with the crowd. "I serve a living, loving God," she confidently declared. "If not for Him or Compassion, neither I, nor certainly not my baby, would be alive today." She went on to explain the loving care and instruction she had received from the CSP staff, nurses, and social workers, who showed her how to improve pre-natal health via exercise, nutrition, and supplements. Then, after her son was born, the encouraging practical lessons—like proper breast-feeding, preventive vaccines, immunizations, and other medicines—have continued.

On a subsequent tour through the CSP wing of the project, we saw cribs, tiny chairs, baby swings, scooters, tricycles, a huge supply of learning toys and instruments, exercise mats, building blocks, and everything else you would see in a well-run education-based nursery. They even had weekly classes for social interaction/training and early literacy. For these moms (who come from households where the average monthly income is perhaps forty dollars at best), this is a sanctuary for their babies in the truest sense of the word. The CSP Director, Rose, explained how the tots were regularly weighed, measured, and examined, to make sure they were within healthy parameters. There was a full pharmaceutical closet with everything a young mother would need for their child. Extensive files were kept on each mom and baby that was regularly updated with the weekly visits at their homes as well as at the project. We were thoroughly impressed. And the results were obvious in the shiny eyes, gleeful giggles, and yes, even the healthy full-throat wails of some of these little nippers.

We saw the wall charts that were proudly displayed showing the progress of each and every infant that had come through the program... and not a single one had died. In fact, once the three-year-olds "graduate" from CSP, they then become eligible for Compassion's regular child sponsorship that runs from pre-K all the way through their late teens. And all of them are thankfully enrolled there to this day.

"What an ongoing blessing we have seen, as Compassion has been involved here for over a generation," said Rev. Thebaud, the aging pastor who had formed the church three decades ago. "So many more precious little ones have been saved physically and spiritually since we began partnering with you. I am retiring soon and will probably be going to be with the Lord very soon as well... however; I can rest easy knowing that things have changed so much for the better from when we started back in 1985."

Outside the project, we saw a few much-healthier-looking kindergartners sailing their tattered kites. And they were in their school uniforms, with good shoes on their feet. I always like asking these little Haitian dynamos their names. It swells my heart every time to hear them proudly blurt out their moniker: "Pierre!" "Camille!" "Sebastien!" "Monique!" "Alain!" "Simone!" "Yves!" I close my eyes and see a skinny tyke waving big ears of corn, yelling out, "Horele!"

And when I asked the mothers that day to introduce their littlest ones, there wasn't a single "Ti Chape" answer in the bunch.

CHAPTER 26

OH, YA GOT TROUBLE

After a month of recovery time last May, my sister Joyce and I decided it was best to move Dad down to Nashville where I could better take care of him. We split responsibilities so that she handles all of his retirement accounts, banking, taxes, and paper work. I will help him with day-to-day stuff. Lots of research and scouting led me to find a lovely retirement community just four miles from my home. They have an excellent staff, great food, and lots of amenities that he did not have in Pennsylvania... including a pool table.

> *Well, either you're closing your eyes*
> *To a situation you do now wish to acknowledge*
> *Or you are not aware of the caliber of disaster indicated*
> *By the presence of a pool table in your community*
> *Ya got trouble, my friend, right here*
> *I say, trouble right here in River City*
> ("Ya Got Trouble" from *The Music Man*, 1959)

So, for the fourth time in less than three years since Mom's passing, we had to sift through his belongings yet again, to prepare for the 600-mile move to his new single-room efficiency apartment. Despite being uprooted from so many extended family and friends in those western PA foothills, Dad was doing pretty well with the concept of being closer to me.

The second day after getting Dad moved in, he wanted to give billiards a whirl. This was another of those games where Dad would regularly defeat me growing up. As the years progressed, I was able to catch up, primarily because—in my senior year of college—there was a table in the lounge directly beneath my dorm room, and nightly games sharpened my skills with banking, angles, and touch. I'm no Minnesota Fats, but I can hold my own.

And all week long your River City youth will be fritterin' away
I say your young men'll be fritterin'!
Fritterin' away their noontime, suppertime, chore time too!
Get the ball in the pocket
Never mind gettin' dandelions pulled
Or the screen door patched or the beefsteak pounded
Never mind pumpin' any water
'Til your parents are caught with the cistern
Empty on a Saturday night
And that's trouble
Oh, yes we got lots and lots of trouble
("Ya Got Trouble" from *The Music Man*, 1959)

It was good to see Dad moving around the green, summing up his options. He was having some difficulty getting balls to drop, but at least he knew what he was trying to do. The same was happening in checkers... and he even started beating me again on the red and black grid. I couldn't have been a happier loser.

Then in August, he had another stroke. I don't think this one was as severe as in April... but it laid him up in the hospital and physical therapy unit for over a month. Recovery came more quickly this time, but it was decided that we should relocate Dad from the assisted living wing to the "Alzheimer's neighborhood" at the home, since he was having some fairly regular bouts with memory issues. But by late summer, it was hard to see any marked difference physically. I was able to start taking him to church regularly; we went to some Nashville Sounds baseballs games and to outings at Centennial Park and Radnor Lake.

As the seasons changed from fall into winter, Dad continued to grow stronger. His appetite was back, and he began regaining the fifteen pounds he had lost from the strokes. When Joyce came down for Christmas, he partook in some marathon Domino and Uno sessions as well as beating both of us in checkers. We went to several Christmas programs at area churches, took part in carol singing, and attended a Predators' hockey game.

With the help of the staff at the facility, my Dad began a morning devotional series a few days a week. It has now grown into a seven-day-a-week ritual every morning at 9:30 and has helped him keep his pastoral gifts in play. They have been working through various books of the Bible and are currently in Acts. Despite his suspect sense of melody, he even leads that regular group of around twenty participants in hymn-sings each morning as well.

The activities at the home also help Dad in his improvement. He's part of a daily group that meets for lunch and discussion on current issues. He takes part in their field trips to area museums, picnics, and tours. He's also a regular in the physical therapy workouts and arts/crafts room.

We've tried out quite a few local eateries on our own, too. Whether it's the spaghetti bolognese at California Pizza Kitchen, the breakfast bar at Shoney's, the meatloaf at Ruby Tuesday's, the chicken teriyaki at Chinatown, the Philly Cheesesteak at Noshville Deli, the pork chops at Calhoun's, a quality cheeseburger at Five Guys, or the milkshakes at TCBY, Dad loves getting out to try new culinary experiences a couple of times each week.

So, here we are thirteen months after the first stroke and nine months after the second, and Dad is doing so well that all of his various medical specialists are quite pleased. In fact, his cancer specialist feels that it is unnecessary for him even to return for regular check-ups anymore. "I see no noticeable traces of cancer in his bloodstream at all, so it is silly to keep coming in here," she said with a huge smile, which Dad reciprocated.

His ticker is in solid shape. His lungs are good. His blood pressure is terrific. His motor skills have improved. His strength has returned (the only time he uses a wheelchair is when we visit the hospital and there are long walks through the facility). We've even found the right blend of decongestants to help him have some respite from the terrible allergy strains that curse the Cumberland Valley.

The new phone I got for Dad—which has volume control in the receiver so he can better hear in his conversations—has been a real plus. This has helped greatly in his communication with friends around the country. His handwriting has even returned enough that he has begun writing cards and letters. I also help him send out an e-mail newsletter every few months to former churches that gives updates on what he's thinking and doing. This always stimulates a fresh round of correspondence from former parishioners.

His sense of humor has started to surface more regularly again. The bad puns, the seemingly endless array of dog jokes, the good-natured teasing.

Mothers of River City!

Heed the warning before it's too late!

Watch for the telltale sign of corruption!

Is there a dime novel hidden in the corncrib?

Is he starting to memorize jokes from Capt. Billy's Whiz Bang?

Are certain words creeping into his conversation?

Words like "swell?"

And, "So's your old man?"

("Ya Got Trouble" from *The Music Man*, 1959)

If I'm not traveling, I see Dad every day. At least three times a week, we head up to the third floor for several games of billiards. Sometimes we play doubles with Isaac and Joe, two other retirees at the home; usually it is just Dad and me, though. Normally I win, but Dad at least averages sinking about five balls per game.

I am glad to report that last week, Pops beat me soundly by six. It didn't hurt that there were a couple of ladies from the home in the parlor watching. There was a real spring in his step as he circled the felt surface—and later, as we returned to his room, he had an air of confidence about him.

We played again yesterday after my return from Cleveland. Dad even had a bit of a swagger as he tauntingly reminded me of the final score from earlier in the week. Why, with a twinkle in his eye, he even started singing Professor Harold Hill's warning as he twisted some chalk to his cue...

Oh, we've got trouble

We're in terrible, terrible trouble

That game with the fifteen numbered balls is a devil's tool!

Oh yes we got trouble, trouble, trouble!

With a capital "T"!

That rhymes with "P"!
And that stands for Pool!

I'll rack 'em up, Dad... It's your break.

Chapter 27

Pounding Rocks

I have a photo hanging over my desk in a forest green frame that nicely accents the aqua-blue bandana and almond skin of the subject: poised with a hammer in striking position above her head, surrounded by piles of battleship-gray granite and withered clusters of nyctanthes bushes... also known as Trees of Sorrow.

It's been a frustrating several weeks with my job... not because of the trip to Brazil—which was stunning—nor the last minute plans for my inaugural visit to Ethiopia. Neither has it been a hassle to see so many needy kids getting life-changing help through the radio events I've helped organize and implement. That part of my work is satisfying beyond compare. But there have been issues having to do with management and direction that have gotten me down... even perturbed.

This is why I have this visage of Anjali hovering above my computer. I'll never forget meeting her three years ago, in a searing 104-degree heat along the dusty two-lane highway between Chennai and Kamaraj Nagar in southeastern India. I had noticed her swinging away as we drove by at 7:30 in the morning and asked our driver if we'd be able to stop and visit with her on our way back

later that afternoon. I was curious about what exactly she was doing, and I made a mental note of landmarks so we wouldn't dash
past her on our return.

Sure enough, at 5:30 PM, we pulled up across the road from her,
and she was still pounding away. Several of us poured out of the
Range Rover, stretching our legs and backs from the cramped quar-
ters... squinting at the relentless glare of the summer sun and oppressive heat that slapped us like a steaming towel as we vacated
the A.C. of the van.

Our guide and primary interpreter, Helen, accompanied us as
we strolled up to this woman who appeared to be in her golden
years. She was hunched over in that all-too-familiar squat position that one sees nearly everywhere in the developing world. She
swung one of several hammers in her repertoire, decisively frac-
turing shoebox-sized chunks of granite into smaller shards. On that
100-foot stretch of land that hugged the pitted asphalt of the roadway, that determined little lady had a dozen piles—each at least
four feet high—of various sized pieces of gravel. Some as small as
a marble... other mounds graduating up to about tangerine circumference.

She was pleasantly flustered by the interruption. My guess is
that she rarely ever spoke to anyone in this lonesome outpost. We
introduced ourselves, and she painfully straightened herself upward and extended a gristled, leathery hand of greeting to each of
us. "I am Anjali. I'm honored to meet you. How may I serve you?"

"We are here to see what God is doing in your beautiful land," I
answered. "As we were driving along to visit a church school where
many children are being assisted, we couldn't help but be fascinated
by what we saw you doing here."

"Oh, that is so wonderful. I have four children of my own, although they are getting older now. As you can see, I break rocks for

a gravel company," the smiling woman stated, as sweat glistened on her neckline. "They take these different size stones that I cut and use them in driveways and walls for rich people's homes and offices."

John, one of our group members, asked, "How many hours each day do you do this?"

"Twelve hours," she meekly responded.

Tracey queried, "How many days a week?"

Anjali looked quizzically at Helen as she translated the question in Hindi. She looked at Tracey with a furrowed brow as if to say, "I don't understand?" Helen then rephrased the question.

"Oh..." Anjali replied, when she comprehended. "I work every day."

"Seven days a week?!" Tracy looked incredulous.

"Yes... I work every day."

Donald asked: "Do you ever get time off for your children?"

"Well... I got to take off four days for the births of my four children... but other than that, I've been blessed with good health, so I never miss work."

John interjected, "How many years have you been doing this?"

Anjali paused, staring off at an unseen calendar in her mind. "Let's see... I think it has been twenty-eight years now. Yes. Twenty-eight years," she said proudly.

Then Tharren politely posed: "If you don't mind me asking, Anjali, how much do you get paid?"

With dancing eyes she beamed, "I earn fifty rupees a day."

We had been in the country long enough to do some quick math in each of our heads. Her backbreaking labor was earning her the equivalent of $1.07 for each twelve-hour day... about $7.49 each week. A rousing $389 per year... a grand total of about $11,000 in nearly three decades.

We stood motionless, staring at our shoes.

After an awkward silence from us, she brightly exclaimed, "I am so happy that I have a job!"

You could've knocked us over with a feather.

"I hope this is not considered rude, Helen, but could you ask her how old she is?" Verne politely queried.

"I will be forty-eight in September," she replied, through her broken smile and chiseled, sun-burnt features. She looked at least twenty years older.

She proudly told us about her children and husband and about where she lived, three miles away. She asked our names and about our families and how we were enjoying our time in her country. When asked about the heat, she said it was better than the days during monsoon season when it rained constantly and she would blister and chafe more easily.

We had to keep ahead of the building traffic flow in the sprawling metropolis of five million in Chennai's teeming streets, so Helen told us we needed to leave. One out of our group slipped Anjali a 1,000-rupee note as we were saying our goodbyes. As we climbed into the van, we looked back to see her eyes about to pop out of her head when she unfolded the currency. She waived wildly, yelled blessings, and blew kisses as we drove away.

We sat silently in the jostling bus for a while... humbled by whom we had just met. Our conversation hadn't lasted more than five minutes... but we knew we would never forget her.

So, as I am grousing about some irritating disappointment with my job, I sit under the visage of Anjali busting up rocks.

I say another prayer for her. And ask for forgiveness.

CHAPTER 28

MERCY IN MATHERE VALLEY

I met a little girl in Kenya twelve days ago. I'm not sure I'll ever be able to get her out of my mind's eye: agonizingly shy, utterly quiet, and a countenance void of expression. She wasn't even four years old, but she was all alone...

Having criss-crossed every time zone on the planet in my humanitarian work and having spent time in all but one continent (Australia), I've seen my share of intense poverty.

I've seen it in the muddy tidal plain undercutting the stilted shacks in Guayaquil, Ecuador... the stifling heat rising off the packed streets of New Dehli, India... the putrid odors of waste that permeate the old slaughterhouse district of Arusha, Tanzania, known as the Hyena Zoo... the seemingly never-ending wave-after-wave of squatter barrios surrounding the world's largest metropolitan sprawl (over thirty million) in Mexico City... the rotting bamboo and child sex-trade of Bangkok's red light district... These are just some of the epicenters where the downward cycle of poverty churns into a deep vortex. It's as if the underground reservoir of Hell is breaking through the surface in certain areas, and everything within miles gets sucked into its hopeless realm.

Even though I have developed the ability to experience it, I have never grown used to it. The intense odors of open sewers, rotting refuse, charcoal pits, and yes—even decaying flesh—burns the eyes and nostrils, often bringing me to the brink of nausea. And always to the verge of tears. But I soldier on, usually because I am leading a group of less-experienced observers, and I try to keep a stiff upper lip and an even keel so as to keep everyone's attitudes up.

But none of this background prepared me for the Methere Valley slum of Nairobi, Kenya.

Can you imagine 700,000 people crammed into an area the size of downtown Nashville? Approximately two miles in length and one mile wide. The lot on which my Tennessee home sits is 50' x 150'. That same space in Methere Valley would house 100 dwellings and close to 500 souls. Over two-thirds of the population is under the age of fourteen, and there are at least 100,000 orphans there due to the forty-percent HIV/AIDS infection rate. Estimates are that one person dies there every six minutes.

As we navigated those streets with no names and even ventured back into the myriad narrow walkways (usually no more than two feet wide), we were told by our Compassion International guide, Moses, to watch out for "flying toilets." Since there is no plumbing in Methere, people often relieve themselves in plastic bags and simply toss them out their window. If you're not struck, you can certainly run the risk of stepping into untold millions of these literal fanny packs that are scattered everywhere and hanging from jagged tin roofing. Gullies have been dug between every cluster of shacks, and they all dribble urine, excrement, and waste water down toward the Methere River, which has long been choked with every sordid swill that mankind can create.

We were fortunate to be visiting during winter season in central Africa. Temperatures had been quite pleasant at seventy-five degrees each day, yet there were still abundant flies and mosquitoes everywhere in that breezeless valley. One could only shake his head wondering what it must feel and smell like when the heat index rises to 110 degrees; the humidity so thick that there is a constant beige cloud hanging over the dank slum.

There was nary a tree or shrub. Not one of us saw even a single blade of grass. Everything was variations of brown... from the rusted metallic scraps that made up most of the housing, to the rutted, constantly muddy pathways. Everyone's limited wardrobe even had a brown tint due to the soiled water it was washed in.

I've said before that Compassion International's child development centers are often akin to a beacon of light on a darkened shore. This was never truer than with the project we visited here. This church school is literally life-giving for the 390 children who are sponsored. They receive their only balanced meal of each day. They are blessed with a school uniform and the only pair of shoes they own. They are given malarial medicines, anti-retroviral treatments for HIV/AIDS, vaccines, vitamins, and regular health and dental check-ups. They receive additional tutoring to assist with their public education. These children know they can't skip their regular school and still be part of the sponsorship program, so there is a zeal for education in this place. They receive additional skill training in areas like baking, carpentry, and even computer technology, to give them opportunities to find employment beyond their otherwise bleak futures.

They have a safe haven for recreation—an actual playground the size of two tennis courts. It's the only open space of this type in this quadrant of the slum. It is *sanctuary* in the truest sense of the word. A shelter where kids are allowed (and encouraged) to be kids. There's even a Scout program where boys and girls are learning disciplines and earning merit badges. What pride this group exhibited as they marched for us and demonstrated their teamwork! Other children sang for us, danced, put on skits, and recited dozens of Bible verses loaded with God's love, hope, and redemption. The scripture is definitely a "living word" in this context, I can assure you.

Amidst all the ceremony and celebration, I noticed this tiny girl for the first time. She was pensively taking it all in. While other children were sprinting, jumping and gleefully punctuating the air with joyous laughter, this muted munchkin stayed anchored in a doorway to one of the classrooms. The orange knit cap and green jacket she was wearing were too large for her, accentuating her small stature. She had cocoa skin, and her big egg-white eyes with coal black centers showed much about her observant little mind.

When they broke us up into groups to play various games, I noticed her again across the courtyard—a silent sentry at her post. Expressionless, but obviously intrigued. Still waters run deep; I began wondering what she might be harboring.

While we were lead around to the various classrooms, the assembly hall, the kitchen, and the bathrooms (this is the only place the kids can actually take a shower), my eyes kept drifting back to the waif who was all by her lonesome. As we were given snacks of cookies and orange Fanta, I excused myself and took some over to her. After much prodding, she eventually grasped a cookie but was hesitant about the drink. My efforts to communicate with her fell on seemingly deaf ears, although our gaze did connect a time or two.

Over the years, I have heard that one of the worst side effects to the scourge of AIDS in Africa is the ridiculous belief that the only way for a man to rid himself of the disease is to have intercourse with a virgin. Since nearly every girl of menstruating age has been with a man, they have now begun raping younger and younger girls, hoping to be "cleansed" of this curse in the process. I can think of no more sordid or cruel lie from the pit of Hell than this. If people think there is no real evil in the world, they simply have not seen the effects of this malicious untruth in action. According to what we were told, in any given week, some of these sweet kids could have actually been raped on their way to the project. Moses told me that with awareness and better security, it is now happening to just a few each week... it used to be much worse.

Could this be what had happened to this innocent child? I asked one of the teachers about her. Shaking her head, she said, "This precious one has experienced way too much. She's an orphan living with her older cousins. We're pretty sure she's been raped; she has most certainly seen too much horror for someone her age to process... That is why she is so quiet. We just try to be patient with her and love her." We were then interrupted before I could ask more. It was time for the closing ceremony and goodbyes.

Hundreds of children gathered in a huge circle around the edge of the playground. Our group of seventeen American radio professionals was interspersed along with other Compassion staff. I convinced my little friend to take my hand and join me. The project leader stood in the center and began singing a chorus on which all the children joined in. It was one of those addictive African melodies with an accented backbeat. Within moments, we were all repeating a joyous dance step in cadence. One by one, he grabbed various ones of us from the visiting party to join him in free form expressions of dance in the center. All the children, the parents, and the teachers, were cheering at our clumsy choreography.

When the leader came to get me, I hoisted the little girl into my arms and proudly strutted into the dancing core: swaying, spinning, and dipping her. We were all singing with abandon and grooving in this communal act of acceptance and worship. I never heard my precious cargo sing, giggle, or even coo. But as we were getting on our bus, one of the teachers told me they had seen her smile for just a fleeting moment—for the first time since she'd become part of the project and had gotten a sponsor six months before.

I bent down to say my goodbyes. I had continued trying to converse with her numerous times during the day... with no results. I told her again, "My name is Mark. I want to pray for you, sweetie. Can you please tell me your name, so I can pray for you?"

Finally, she parted her lips, and I heard the faintest of squeaks.

I leaned in close and said, "Could you say that again, please?"

"Mercy. My name is Mercy," she whispered.

I cried in my hotel room the rest of that evening as I searched my Bible for some solace.

*But in your great **mercy** you did not put an end to them or abandon them, for you are a gracious and merciful God.* (Nehemiah 9:31)

*Do not hold against us the sins of the fathers; may your **mercy** come quickly to meet us, for we are in desperate need.* (Psalms 79:8)

*This is what the LORD Almighty says: Administer true justice; show **mercy** and compassion to one another.* (Zechariah 7:9)

*He has shown you, O man, what is good. And what does the LORD require of you? To act justly and to love **mercy** and to walk humbly with your God.* (Micah 6:8)

*But for that very reason I was shown **mercy** so that in me, the worst of sinners, Christ Jesus might display his unlimited patience as an example for those who would believe on him and receive eternal life.* (I Timothy 1:16)

*Jesus said, "Go home to your family and tell them how much the Lord has done for you, and how He has had **mercy** on you."* (Mark 5:19)

*The LORD has heard my cry for **mercy**; the LORD accepts my prayer.* (Psalms 6:9)

CHAPTER 29

ENTERTAINING ANGELS

It's been an extraordinary twelve hours. I've come down with bronchitis, and the deep coughing fits late at night have made it difficult to sleep. Having just finished Philip Yancey's wonderful book: *Prayer: Does It Make Any Difference?* I decided to put some of its ideas into motion last night when slumber was slow in coming.

My dear friend Katy—an independent artist getting ready for a tour—has been staying in my den this week to help conserve her funds. She's one of the most "thought-full" people I know, and we always have stimulating conversations. Last evening was no different. I could tell she was burdened about something, and she began to confide about some heart-rending decisions she is trying to make. Being very cognizant of not wanting to repeat some of the same actions earlier in her life that still carry repercussions today, she was encumbered and weary from all the internal dialogue. And she was also finding it hard to pray because of potential pain that might come from any number of scenarios that could unfold.

But we prayed anyway.

It was into the early hours of the morning when we finished sharing, and I took more cough medicine, hoping for the best as I crawled into my bed. It soon became apparent that it was going to be another restless night. Rather than mope and whine between coughing fits, I decided to focus my energy on Katy's situation... simply asking God to extend additional grace her way: to assure her of His love, to grant her clarity and resolve, to foster peace in her heart, and most of all, to envelope her in His loving arms.

Finally, around 4 AM, I drifted into a half-slumber, and a vivid dream ensued. Without going into a lot of detail, let me just say that it was full of divine encouragement and warmth toward those who are burdened. As God's concern shone down on her, I saw Katy lay aside her hindrance, give up her straining, and simply bask in the tender acceptance He offers... being overwhelmed by His great fondness for her as she gazed upward into that light and felt His eternal embrace.

I awoke from the dream and immediately had a scripture verse come to mind. My Dad used to end many of his sermons with this... but I hadn't consciously thought of it in at least a decade. I hopped out of bed, scurried up the stairs to my office where I keep my study Bible, and looked it up just to make sure it existed as I remembered it:

May the Lord bless you and keep you
May the Lord make His face to shine upon you
And be gracious to you
May the Lord turn His face toward you
And give you peace
(Numbers 6:24-26)

I went back to my bed, and— between coughing fits—excitedly continued to pray for Katy, as the dawn began creeping into my bedroom window.

A few hours passed, and I decided to go ahead and get up. Katy had agreed to follow me to a mechanic's where I was to leave my car for transmission work, so we set out across town to fight rush hour traffic at 7:30. Oddly enough, the roads were pretty clear on both ends of the trip. During the return back, the subject of the previous night came up again. I mentioned to her that—due to the congestion in my chest—I had been unable to sleep, but that I had been inspired to keep praying for her. I told her of the subsequent dream and the scripture that came to me.

She was consoled by what I shared... It was one of those moments where you felt like you were being a conduit of something God was trying to impart to someone else. He works in unique ways like that.

Katy needed to tackle some other errands, and as she dropped me off at the house, we both noticed a homeless woman who had been knocking on the door of my neighbors' home without any success. When the lady saw me, she called out to see if I could be of help.

As is my custom with street people, I ask God for split second confirmation in these encounters... and this time it was a gentle, "Yes—help her." So I motioned for her to come on over.

The African-American woman was disheveled in a slapdash array of filthy garments, and she was laboring heavily while she walked. As she approached my steps, I could see that her skin was somewhat discolored, and she had a significant amount of snot dripping down her nose and around her mouth. Through garbled and winded speech, she tried to tell her story—a conglomeration of snippets about wanting to help her babies get some food, her own schizophrenia, and being frustrated about taking so long to find shelter for herself the previous night, which had been one of the coldest of the season so far—down into the teens.

"My name is Mark," I said as I extended my hand.

She eyed me cautiously, then took the tattered mitten off her right hand and shook it. "I... I'm... I'm Gwen," she stuttered.

I asked if she would like to come in. She was somewhat leery.

"M-m-mo-most folks won't even come to the door—and n-no-nobody wants to ask me in." She seemed very hesitant.

But I coaxed her inside. "Would you like some breakfast? I just got back from my friend taking me to get my car repaired, and I was going to fix some."

"Uhh... ummm... sure," she stammered.

I ushered her into the kitchen and asked what she might like. Cereal, toast, and hot chocolate were her choices. We chatted about where she was from (Houston), her children (she had three, aged six months, three years, and six years), where she was staying most nights (The Nashville Rescue Mission for Women—but it was full by the time she got there last night, so she found a cousin a few blocks away who was willing to let them sleep on her floor).

She felt compelled to show me her TennCare medications for schizophrenia, as well as her ID bracelet and prescription forms. I've certainly learned much about various scams that homeless sorts like to perpetrate on well-meaning people, having learned the hard way with several instances over the years. And I often call them on it when they try various charades on me. But I still help and even house various vagabonds when I sense God wants me to... and I felt that He truly wanted me to be there for this woman on this day... no matter how odd some of her circumstances seemed to be.

When I asked about the father of her children, she said, "R-Rob-Robert died last year. He had AIDS." With a long pause, she then blurted out, "I... I... h-h-have AIDS, too."

I sighed and leaned against my counter as I heard her misery. *Why do some have to suffer so much, Lord?* I prayed to myself. Gathering my composure, I offered, "Oh, Gwen... I am so sorry about your loss and about the pain you're going through."

Before I could ask about her children, she piped in: "My kids are OK, thank God. I-I-I'm working h-h-hard on getting things set up for them once I'm gone." She then pulled up her right pant leg to show me the appendage that was no bigger around than my arm and covered in raw sores... then showed the same with her left arm. "As you can see, M-M-Mr. Mark, I probably don't have m-m-much time."

Having been around this scourge of our age at AIDS Hospices here in the States, as well as seeing it so prevalently amongst the poor of the African plains, I am not taken aback in the least in these situations. I pulled a chair next to hers as she ate, and I put my arm on her shoulder and squeezed it lightly. She meekly smiled at me through cheeks filled with corn flakes. What tension there was in the air melted away while we continued to visit.

As we were finishing breakfast, I asked if she needed any more food for the remainder of the day. "That would sho 'nuff be very k-k-kind, Mr. Mark" she said. I asked her to choose from my sandwich supplies and made some up for her and her kids. I brewed some more hot cocoa and put it into one of those warmth-holding sippy-cups for her to keep. Noticing that she only had a flimsy sweater and a thin wind-breaker jacket, I asked if she'd like some additional clothing. I gave her some sweat pants, sweatshirts, four pairs of socks, and a scarf my grandmother had knitted. I also gave her an overnight bag with a carrying strap to put all her belongings in rather than the torn plastic grocery sacks she was using. It was a gift from my job, and had "Compassion" embroidered on the side.

Reading it, she said, "Th-tha-that there is one of the most God-blessed words there is." Knowing that it comes from the two Latin-root words: "to suffer," and "with," I was beginning to fight back tears.

She then asked, "Mr. Mark, you're a Christian, aren't you?"

"Yes, I try to follow Jesus... He's the only reason I can make any sense out of this messed-up world," I replied.

"Me too," she declared. She then stated something very profound: "Y-y-you lost someone you loved very much two summers ago, didn't you?"

I paused from packing the bag and looked straight into her eyes. "Why yes... My mother died two July's ago from stomach cancer."

"U-hmmm," she nodded. "I know she's very proud of you and what you do for other folks."

I was dumbfounded. How on earth... ?

"Mr. Mark, w-w-would you pray with me before I go?"

We both sat down, and I pulled my chair facing hers and placed both of her scab-covered hands in mine. I labored through my own cough, runny nose and salty eyes—accentuated by more than just my illness—and asked our loving Savior to help Gwen and her children, to meet their needs, and to protect them.

When I finished, she squeezed my hands and prayed in a very soft voice... of one who felt very familiar with her beloved: "Thank you so much Jesus, for loving me and my children. Thank you for helping us find a place to sleep last night. Thank you for these kind provisions Mr. Mark has blessed us with." Her stuttering was nearly non-existent as she talked sweetly with her Lord.

Gwen then clenched my hands even tighter and began to recite something obviously very near and dear to her heart: "May the Lord bless you and keep you. May the Lord make His face to shine upon you and be gracious to you. May the Lord turn His face toward you and give you peace. Amen."

I was nearly in a state of shock as we both stood up. I pulled her close and gave her a long hug. We were both crying.

As I walked her to the front door and helped her down my porch stairs, I told her to please come by again should she need anything. "It was so nice to meet you, Mr. Mark. May the Lord continue to bless this house." She hobbled down the street in the direction where she said her cousin lived.

Closing the front door, I leaned back against it, my face wet with tears. Out of 31,103 verses in the Bible, how did she know to quote those three? How could she have known about my loss? Why was she out pounding on doors at 8 AM on a frigid January morning? Why had there been virtually no traffic during that time and I arrived at just the moment she was next to my house?

Sometimes answers are too wonderful to be hindered by questions, or perhaps it is within those questions that we are most fully alive.

Chapter 30

Through Your Hands

As a little tyke, I would sometimes crawl into my Dad's lap while he'd read the evening paper or watch television. Fascinated with the size of his hands, I would play with his fingers and thumbs, comparing them to mine. The grooves, wrinkles, and intricate detail of the rope-like bands of his fingerprints were so much more distinct than the smooth skin on my little mitts. The patches of hair on his knuckles and the back of his fists were dark compared to the peach fuzz on mine. I would press my miniature digits against his and wonder if mine would ever be as big.

I remember how his paw wrapped around mine as he stood behind me and taught how to grip a bat...his left on mine over the left handlebar and his right on my lower back as he ran alongside and steadied me while I learned to balance a bicycle without training wheels...the firm slap of his flattened right palm as he gave me ten good whacks on my behind for being disobedient...his hand patting gently on my the back of my neck as he leaned over my shoulder to help me with a tough bout of algebra homework...and his arm wrapped around my side and proudly embracing me upon my graduation from Wheaton.

The very week that the final draft of this manuscript was edited and the graphic design for this cover was approved, Dad started slipping away.

A month earlier, he had fallen and broken his hip while walking to the dining hall at his retirement home. His vertigo had become more pronounced in the past year, causing him to fracture his forearm from a spill while taking off his shoes and to crack his lower right arm from a tumble while taking a shower. The resultant physical therapy from these first two setbacks went well. But he was not responding at all to the special hospital care he was receiving after his hip needed rebuilding.

Dad's appetite was receding. He was becoming borderline dehydrated. We were doing all in our power to help him, but it was becoming obvious that he was winding down. The morning his kidneys started failing, I called Joyce—on business in Washington DC—and she was able to catch a flight that would arrive by late afternoon.

He was wavering in and out of consciousness, but in the moments where Dad seemed coherent, I grabbed his hand and told him Joyce was on her way. "Can you hold on long enough to see her?" I asked with a catch in my throat. "She really wants to say goodbye." His eyes connected with mine, and he nodded slightly. Then his lids closed and never reopened as he began descending into a more comatose state.

I eased my hand into his and waited. That tactile intertwining brought back memories of my little hand in his from five decades ago. For the first time, I realized how similar they now looked. Sure, his were more weathered...a few liver spots here and there, and the hairs were now all gray...but still showed equal measures of strength, character, and gentleness that I can only hope to emulate.

In the last few years, with all the time we had sharing meals and driving around, we had some conversations that I will always treasure. These talks were washing over me now. I remembered sharing with him some of my insecurities, and he confessed several episodes of his own...how in his college days, he woke up in a hung-over haze inside his car in front of his apartment—after driving home drunk—wondering how the hell he had navigated traffic in that state, and his hands trembled on the steering wheel as dawn burned his bloodshot eyes. While he practically crawled up the stairs with nausea, he swore that he would not end up like his dad. That moment helped lead him to search seriously for better reasons to live.

He told me of flipping through scriptures searching for answers and clasping his hands tightly together in prayer asking Christ into his life. He recalled his sweaty palms raking through his hair several years after that, as he paced back and forth trying to make a decision about going into the ministry.

"I can still distinctly remember holding each one of you in my arms after you were born," he had told me. "I was feeling so unworthy of the honor. I especially recollect Joyce... cupping the back of her tiny, perfect little head in the meat of my hand—her big blue eyes gazing up at me. 'Lord,' I prayed, 'How can I possibly provide for these three beautiful children you have given to Marilyn and me?' My salary wasn't even $10,000 a year back then, and there were so many responsibilities in leading a church."

Still you argue for an option
Still you angle for your case
Like you wouldn't know a burning bush
If it blew up in your face
Yeah, we scheme about the future
And we dream about the past

When just a simple reaching out

Might build a bridge that lasts

("Through Your Hands" by John Hiatt from *Stolen Moments*, 1990)

Mulling these images over for several hours, I was simultaneously praying that God would allow my sister to travel without delay. Katy volunteered to pick Joyce up at the airport and they raced through early evening rush hour traffic. Dad's breathing had become very erratic, and he was wincing in agitation from the turmoil that was wreaking mayhem intestinally.

When she arrived, Sis swept into the room and spoke in her upbeat manner, "I'm here now, Dad. So very happy to be with you." As she slipped her hand into his, he squeezed hard and would not let go for the next ninety minutes.

The doctor on duty, Heather, felt that Dad was very near the end. We wanted to make him as comfortable as possible and asked if they could administer morphine to help with the pain that was burning his stomach. They started doses every few hours.

My home is just two miles away, so I dashed over to get a CD player and some music I knew Dad enjoyed. I brought a Presbyterian hymnal and some clothes and toiletries so we could make ourselves comfortable for however long we would need to be by his side. I also grabbed a couple lamps to give us respite from the stark glare of fluorescent lighting.

The gentleman who had been Dad's roommate for the previous week was discharged earlier that day, and the staff told us we could use the extra bed. We pulled it next to my father's and took turns lying beside him, holding his hand, patting his arm, and gently reassuring him that it was going to be OK. "We're here to help you step over to the other side, Dad."

One album was a collection of hymns sung by Lynda Poston-

Smith entitled *Steal Away Home: Songs of Hope and Comfort.* This had been a favorite of my Mother's, not only for the eclectic selections, but also because their voices were nearly identical. Mom had operatic skill in her beautiful soprano, and the blend of her singing along while she did housework would've caused anyone to think she was Lynda's sister.

"This sounds just like Mom, doesn't it Dad?" I asked. His eyebrows raised up and down as his lips moved silently, trying to sing along. "She's waiting for you, Dad. Mom is calling you home." His grip grew strong around my hand.

You were dreaming on a park bench
'Bout a broad highway somewhere
When the music from the carillon
Seemed to hurl your heart out there
Past the scientific darkness
Past the fireflies that float
To an angel bending down
To wrap you in her warmest coat

("Through Your Hands" by John Hiatt from *Stolen Moments*, 1990)

That night, the staff welcomed Joyce to sleep in the empty room next door. I cozied-beside Dad, our shoulders touching, caressing his arm, putting my hand on his chest when his breathing became agitated. "You're doing fine, Dad. You can make this trip at your own pace," I whispered.

I had gotten him some of his beloved A&W Root Beer, and would dip swabs of the sweet brew to wet his lips every half hour or so. Sometimes he would even swallow. "Nothing like a cold root beer, huh, Dad?" I would ask, and sometimes his eyebrows would rise in response.

As the hours melted one into another, a certain cadence took over his air intake: a large inhale, a slight moan, and then a sustained exhale. I began to wonder which one might be his last. I didn't want to let him go, but he had been longing to for months. At least a dozen times in that stretch, he admitted that he wanted to go to heaven. "I've had enough, Mark, and I don't think I've got anything left to give anyway," he lamented.

Why is it that so often as life winds down, there is such grayness to it?

When half-light started seeping through the window at sunup, the morphine must've been pretty well integrated into his system, as his breathing had become even-paced with no external signs of pain. Vitals were fairly stable. So once Joyce was alert and in the room, I drove home to eat and shower.

While I was gone, she pulled out the hymnal and began singing to Dad while sitting with him hand-in-hand. On certain numbers, he would twitch in recognition. She went cover-to-cover, singing every one that she remembered: "Children of the Heavenly Father," "Great Is Thy Faithfulness," "Be Thou My Vision," "Like A River Glorious," "All Hail the Power of Jesus' Name," "To God Be The Glory," "Breathe On Me, Oh Breath of God," "Christ the Lord Is Risen Today," "Fairest Lord Jesus," "For the Beauty of the Earth," "Great Is They Faithfulness," "Holy, Holy, Holy," "How Great Thou Art," "Joyful, Joyful, We Adore Thee," "Open My Eyes That I May See," "What a Friend We Have In Jesus," "When I Survey The Wondrous Cross," "Praise Ye The Lord," and "Guide Me, Oh Thou Great Jehovah" were the ones she noted that he acknowledged the most. On some, tears even trickled down his cheeks.

Knowing my sister's ambivalence about much of evangelicalism over the past several decades, this was stirring a reconnection of memories growing up in a pastor's home. The ridiculous pressures, expectations of the fundamental lifestyle, and disappointments over decisions made (or not made) seemed to be of no consequence during this final bond between a daughter and father. These time-tested melodies and hope-filled psalms swept over the both of them. "Blessed Assurance," indeed.

Angels, descending, bring from above
Echoes of mercy, whispers of love
Watching and waiting, looking above
Filled with His goodness, lost in His love
("Blessed Assurance," Fanny Crosby, 1873)

Upon my return, Joyce took a break to have breakfast and shop for some clothes (she had only packed for a two-day business trip). In my next few hours with Dad, I read him some of the newspaper, prayed with him, and recited some portions of scripture.

When Dad seemed to be in a rapt sleep, I pulled out Kathleen Norris' *Acedia and Me*, which I had been working through for the past month. This book is a telling of her discovery and contemplation of acedia, one of the original "Seven Deadly Sins" that over the past five hundred years has been referred to more as "sloth." Even in the past century it has more often been looked at as "depression." Norris ties this in with the long struggle of her husband's declining health over several decades. The chapter I opened that afternoon was entitled "And to the End Arriving." I knew that she was going to eventually talk of his passing, but I had no idea it would be nearly a hundred pages before the close of the dissertation. As I read of her tending to him on his deathbed, barely holding on to life, I found myself eminently encouraged. I sensed the Spirit once again inter-lacing threads of circumstance to show me tender concern.

Kathleen recounted her husband David's favorite prayer, which was the final utterance of the compline (from the Latin "com-plete"—the service used to bring each day to a close): "May the Lord grant us a peaceful night...and a perfect end." I nodded in af-firmation that—in God's mercy—the same would be true for Dad in His timing.

Throughout that afternoon, we pondered moving him to my house for final hospice. His breathing seemed measured and steady, as if he had found a comfortable pace that might sustain him for a while. In and out went the rhythm of life. The expansion of his chest welling with hope, to be followed—as is the nature of all things—with the subsequent sigh of resignation. To be repeated over, and over, and over.

My sister and I took turns sitting with Dad while the other would make calls to loved ones. We imparted courage to him and each other as he made each symbolic step. His vital signs were be-ginning to fluctuate. His lungs started to gather fluid, and we heard occasional deep gurgling sounds in his throat.

In some ways, it was eerily similar to six years earlier when Mom had a massive stroke during her recovery from stout stomach cancer treatments. They were returning to Pittsburgh from a family reunion in Kentucky, when she collapsed at a freeway exit conve-nience store in southeast Ohio. As soon as Dad called us, Joyce and I raced to the hospital she had been taken to in Dayton—each of us covering the 300 miles from Indiana and Tennessee respectively in blazing times.

We had friends from Pennsylvania overnight Mom's favor-ite CD's to us, and we bought a unit to play them for her while we took turns holding her hand and speaking with her. After several tests, the doctors concluded that if she were ever to regain aware-ness, she would most likely have very limited quality of life. Both Mom and Dad had drawn up extremely clear living wills that left no doubt regarding their choice in a situation like this: do not attempt to maintain. We read it and re-read it carefully, met with the physicians, pondered with the hospital chaplain, and prayed separately and communally. After two days, we unanimously decided, with the staff's blessing and cooperation, that we would take Mom off life support. She had been sending us cues, too: her blood pressure was wildly erratic, her body temperature was soaring to 104 degrees; her heart rate was all over the chart.

She was telling us to let her go.

Even though it was a non-religious hospital, nearly every nurse and doctor who had been helping in those three days came into her room when the time arrived. We all held hands and prayed around Mom. Earlier that day, the resident chaplain, Rev. Robinson, had heard us playing Lynda Poston-Smith's version of "Swing Low, Sweet Chariot." After he and Dad prayed for God's presence and blessing as all life-sustaining machinery and fluids were shut down, the clergyman asked that we play it again and sing in unison.

Our voices were quivering but determined as we sang…

Swing low, sweet chariot
Comin' for to carry me home
Swing low, sweet chariot
Comin' for to carry me home

I think the three of us had the same image of Mom singing this in front of thousands at numerous church services where she would give her passionate rendition of her favorite spiritual.

I looked over Jordan
And what did I see?
Comin' for to carry me home

A band of angels comin' after me
Comin' for to carry me home

Dad, who we did not often see cry, was sobbing pretty hard, and I put my arm around him...

Sometimes I'm up, and sometimes I'm down
Coming for to carry me home
But still my soul feels heavenly bound
Coming for to carry me home

We had all figured that with Dad's prostate cancer surgery thirteen years earlier and triple by-pass just six years later, he would be the first to go. Now it was beginning to sink in that Mom was crossing over first...

If you get to heaven before I do
Comin' for to carry me home
Tell all my friends I'm a-comin' too
Comin' for to carry me home
("Swing Low Sweet Chariot" by Wallis Willis, 1850)

We watched the life signs slowly ebb...the color drain from her face. Joyce, Dad, and I all got on our knees next to Mom as the heartbeat grew fainter and fainter.

And she was gone...in just four minutes.

Everyone quietly left us by her body. It was so somber but about as holy as you could want. We were humbled to be there.

So, here were the three of us again, but now Dad was in the reclining and declining position, with Joyce and I on either side of him late on a sun-drenched spring day in Nashville. Dad's breathing was the only sound in the room...despite the occasional quiet chatting as Joyce and I pondered his life.

I contemplated what he had imparted to me—imprinted into my life with his guiding hand of love, discipline, and direction. Each sustained breath seemed to bring another lesson to mind, whether it was how to laugh, accepting those in need, striving for relevance to people's needs, loyalty, standing up for what was right, and care for others above yourself. One bit of wisdom that grew more precious with age was admitting we would never really know all the answers in this life.

As a minister, Dad allowed people to ask hard questions about faith or the lack thereof. His permitting people to be open with their doubts made them more comfortable in hearing possible solutions through scripture and his personal experiences. And he knew that these possible answers often did not come quickly but needed patience for all involved.

I remember him sometimes saying, "There are lots of good preachers out there...but there never seem to be enough pastors." Now Joyce and I were in that place where Dad was when had consoled so many with his amazing bedside manner for those in the hospital. He was a great listener to those who were grieving, knowing when to pray and when to be silent. We were doing our best to reflect that back to him as he lay there. Things had grown peaceful in the midst of the sadness and reflection as the afternoon progressed. The intake and outflow had now become pretty unencumbered and even.

In...out...pause. In...out...pause. And then, without any warning whatsoever, he stopped. No trauma, no struggle, no difficulty. He breathed his last and slipped away.

Joyce and I looked at each other, tears welling. "Good for you, Dad. You did good," she whispered.

There's a healing touch to find you
On that broad highway somewhere
To lift you high
As music flying
Through the angel's hair

("Through Your Hands" by John Hiatt from *Stolen Moments*, 1990)

It dawned on me that we had been given a very rare gift in this modern age: to be by the side of each of our parents when they passed and to see them move so gently from one realm to the next.

Jim was yanked away from us without warning. I could never say goodbyes to Ernie, or John, or Mike back in my college days, nor many others who have departed subsequently. But for the two people who gave me life in the first place—the two who loved me most—I was allowed the honor of seeing them through.

As I held his hand that final time, still warm but beginning to cool as his spirit left him, I remember doing the same with him five years after Mom had died when he was recovering from his broken arm. He was feeling quite low. "Sometimes I wonder what all of my life meant," he confessed. "The toil of my hands...Will there be any lasting impact?" Staring out at a powdered dusk, he paused for a while. "It used to sadden Marilyn and me that none of you brought grandchildren into our lives. But last night the Lord reminded me of what you and Joyce had done—a lot which wouldn't have happened if you had families. Look at the university Joyce is helping start in Africa. That source of higher education is going to change Angola for generations to come. And then there are those 150,000 sponsors you've found for needy kids through radio and concert events with Compassion in these decades you've worked with them."

"You taught and modeled well, Dad." I reminded him. "In so

many ways you showed us how to serve—not just in words, but also actions."

"Yeah," he replied, brightening up. "When you put your hand to the plow, you don't always realize what the harvest will look like until you go through too much rain, too much heat, locusts, beetles, fire ants, and long stretches of wondering if it will amount to much."

We've been flooded with hundreds of testimonies of the impact of Mom and Dad since his passing. At his memorial service in Pittsburgh, as well as via cards, e-mails, and phone calls, we have heard from some of the thousands that were touched over those sixty-plus years of service at the eight congregations they served.

Don't ask what you are not doing
Because your voice cannot command
In time we will move mountains
And it will come through your hands

("Through Your Hands" by John Hiatt from *Stolen Moments*, 1990)

CHAPTER 31

GRAY MATTERS

I hadn't had "The Barrier Dream" in at least a decade, but in the first few days I began working on this text, it returned. That wall that I was being pulled toward was even more immense... something like one would conjure from *Lord of the Rings*. It was not only separating me from my struggle and what might be on the other side, but maybe more importantly, it was serving as a delineation between black and white. It was the junction where the two apparent opposites meet.

As I continued on my journey toward it, trying with all my might not to veer into dark negativity or list headlong into naïve optimism, I knew that the line between them—that center line defined by that splinter of fierce radiance—was my hope. I also noticed that there were others who were trying to get there as well: some ahead of me, some behind—others who had been alongside at one time who had lost their way.

I knew that for me to reach that point, I had to hone in and keep that ray right between my eyes. Keeping on that proverbial "straight and narrow" was proving difficult for me as well. Strong crosswinds, patches of fog, poor traction, sinkholes, washouts, and various splits in the path, were constant reminders of my fallibility in navigation. And most of the ruts of those before me swerved away from what seemed the most direct route. Yet, if I zeroed-in on just the beam, it was too bright for my unaccustomed sight, and it made my vision insensitive to others in my peripheral view.

I realized now that this bastion was the boundary of my temporal life—the limit of understanding. In order to keep my balance, have full stereoscopic vision, and maintain some semblance of focus on that luminous lead, I found myself recalibrating, adjusting, and even squinting at times. Like a navigator on a ship being tossed in rough seas, I tried to find the North Star in between the blurring clouds and make adjustments in course. Every captain learns with experience that there is never a straight line to a destination. There is zigging and zagging based on wind, currents, and seasonal conditions that are quite often unpredictable.

The final time I had the dream, I came within arm's length of the bulwark. It reached so high, I'm not sure I could see the top, and when I looked down its length in each direction, it stretched to what seemed like infinity... all white to my left, all black to my right. And that laser still emanated from the dividing line—a slip so miniscule that it was nearly immeasurable. Even as I attempted to remain centered, if I closed my right eye, all I could see out of my left was white. If I clenched my left, all I saw was black through my right. But I found that with both eyes open as I approached the division, I began to see a mixture of both... a gray that had a brilliant laser of indescribable light cutting through the center.

Faith and doubt are the primary colors that make up gray... They're an admixture that, when applied with an honest heart, can bring a solace that leaning too heavily on one or the other can never bring. It's like muscle and bone. The sinew has no power on its own unless it is tethered and woven around the sturdy base of cartilage.

Likewise, that skeletal structure will utterly collapse in a heap if not interlaced with vigorous tendons. Together, they form a vital, potent force. One really can't function without the other. They need each other. And they are useless if each tries to go solo.

Some Biblical scholars have come to the conclusion that the Book of Job is the oldest of all the texts in the Hebraic lexicon... Indeed, it may be the most ancient of all stories, handed down in a verbal tradition perhaps thousands of years before Moses began compiling. If this is so, then what a way for God to set the stage for His incarnation into this world that He set in motion. Right out of the chute, He makes clear that: "Life is hard. It's unpredictable. It may seem terribly unfair at times, but I will *never* tell you that it *is* fair. There will be deep joy, faith-fullness, familial love, commitment, and abundance offset by bitter disappointment, agony, loneliness and doubt. Many well-meaning people will give you advice—much of it insensitive and even wrong—and this will vex you greatly. And I will allow you the freedom to question Me—even complain about your plight. Ultimately, I will remind you—sometimes gently, at other times sternly—that I am in charge." In that very first epic tale, God sets the standard of grayness and how not only to navigate it... but how to appreciate it.

Philip Yancey has pondered that in depth in his writings. He comes the the conclusion that "One bold message in the Book of Job is that you can say anything to God. Throw him your grief, your anger, your doubt, your bitterness, your betrayal, your disappointment—He can absorb them all. As often as not, spiritual giants of the Bible are shown *contending* with God. They prefer to go away limping, like Jacob, rather than to shut God out. In this respect, the Bible prefigures a tenet of modern psychology: You can't deny your feelings or make them disappear, so you might as well express them. God can deal with every human response save one. He cannot abide the response I fall back on instinctively: an attempt to ignore him or treat him as though he does not exist. That response never once occurred to Job."

Later on, Ecclesiastes was written as a witness to mankind's history of futility in trying to comprehend, and it spotlights my inability to find meaning without God—and often times, even *with* Him. It's necessary gray.

We're fond of quoting all the Psalms about happy lambs and green pastures, but we often forget that nearly 100 of those chapters are Psalms of Lament and Psalms of Complaint. Once again, God is reminding us that faith and doubt are inextricably linked.

In my earlier days, this gray—this in-betweeness—would've caused consternation. The maybes, the not-quite-yets, and the what-just-happeneds, would sometimes throw me off wondering why I couldn't see more clearly. But with experience, I've come to realize that this gray is an indicator that I'm getting closer. By keeping my eyes open wide as I get closer to The Truth, I see that mixture of the black and white. Instead of fearing it, I have come to accept it: even embrace it.

As of yet, I haven't been able to put my nose right into that junction between white and black. Someday it will burn everything away; all that will be left is something non-physical that will be pulled through. I also know now that I'll not have the strength to push myself to the other side. I am being drawn by that Light's own good pleasure. The more I surrender to it, the more content I become. The less I strive to conquer, the more peace I will receive.

And what would the alternative be? Famous atheist Bertrand Russell said, "The center of me is always and eternally a terrible pain... a curious wild pain... a searching for something beyond what the world contains."

In those three years that I was away from faith, I experienced this on a nearly nightly basis. And even now, in my most honest moments, I still contend with it.

That curiosity is brought fully alive in embracing the gray. It is that deep eagerness to know and to be known. "Curiosity is the unknown fruit of the Spirit: the stealthy expression of God's presence," Mike Yaconelli said. "It is the shape of our hunger for God. We question God without apology; we march into the presence of God bringing armfuls of questions—without fear—because God is not afraid of them. People are afraid. Institutions are afraid. But God is not."

He is not afraid because he experienced them in the flesh himself, by partaking personally in our hard questions. "The New Testament portrays a God who, by being wholly present in the dying cry of Jesus of Nazareth, even doubted and questioned himself," says Chesterton. The Artist had to become part of the painting and allow dark colors to be used to attain the ultimate beauty. As Paul Tournier says: "Where there is no longer any opportunity for doubt, there is no longer any opportunity for faith, either."

I gain confidence, because he not only showed me how to suffer, but he overcame it by surrender and sacrifice. Dostoevsky nailed it by confessing, "My Hosanna has come forth through the crucible of doubt."

Parker Palmer puts it this way:

> In the visible world of nature, a great truth is concealed in plain sight; diminishment and beauty, darkness and light, death and life— are not opposites. They are held together in the paradox of hidden wholeness. In a paradox, opposites do not negate each; they cohere in mysterious unity at the heart of reality. But in a culture that prefers the ease of either-or thinking to the complexities of paradox, we have a hard time holding opposites together. We want light without

darkness, the glories of spring and summer without the demands of autumn and winter. When we so fear the dark that we demand light around the clock, there can be only one result: artificial light that is glaring and graceless and, beyond its borders, a darkness that grows ever more terrifying as we try to hold it off. Split off from each other, neither darkness nor light is fit for human habitation. But if we allow the paradox of darkness and light to be, the two will conspire to bring wholeness and health to every living thing.

Even this year, as I have been trying to put the finishing touches on this memoir, I've been swimming in grief from losing ten more friends. Three more are battling intense cancer; another has suffered a debilitating stroke. Each of these is close to me in age. And Dad, who wrestled with more and more depression in his last days, asked me at one point why he should live any longer. All of this—along with increased neck and back pain as the result of deteriorating discs in my spine—has added to the malaise. I was hoping to wrap a nice bow on top of this closing thought, but life isn't quite so tidy and predictable, is it?

Once again… always again, I lean into Christ. He inhabited the gray better than anyone, ever… and he suffered for it. We read often of his "suffering with." He came to partake in our hard questions, and he seemed to have plenty of his own.

Can there be any real knowledge of Christ unless I experience uncertainty, sorrow, pain, and loneliness as well? Just as Jesus presented his doubt and suffering to God, I can do the same, asking him to use it to help me have more concern and deeper empathy for him, for others… and even for myself. I may have to say it through clenched teeth, just as my Lord did in the Garden of Gethsemane in his darkest hours of fear and anxiety. But through surrender comes acceptance.

Accepting this ambiguity may be one of the greatest acts of my fledgling faith. The Cloud of Unknowing surrounds me. I can choose to swing wildly at the mist and expend great energy as I fret about my lack of long-range clarity. But as the years and experiences have continued, I've come to realize that allowing it to envelope me... to embrace it... even to breathe it in—may be the wisest course of action.

As Bono says, "My favorite song is *Amazing Grace*, and my second favorite is *Help Me Make It Through the Night*. And most of the time, I have to let it go at that."

ACKNOWLEDGEMENTS

John Hollingsworth: for being a loving father, demonstrating the heart of a pastor, and for teaching me about social justice; Joyce Hollingsworth for being a such a helpful, caring, dynamic, and wonderfully strange sister; Marilyn Hollingsworth for bringing a passion for art and music into my life...I miss you much; and Jim...sure wish we could've had more time to become brothers again.

A huge thank-you to Katy Kinard for her friendship and encouragement, as well as skill and patience in helping with the editing of this manuscript. Also to Suzanna Spring for her artful design of the cover. Lori Sellstrom and the team at Wheatmark have given solid guidance, and I am grateful for that.

Deep thanks to all my old school chums that have stuck by me through many a decade: Sam Smith, Bill Harris, Randy York, Duke Merrill, Debbie Messinese, Jon Forbes, "Scottone the Only" Whitney, John Wheeler, Butch Maltby, Graf Hilgenhurst, Paul and Barb Barnes, Brian Hug, J.R. and Elaine Lawrence, and Malcolm MacGregor.

So much appreciation for Musoids that have befriended me along the way: Doug Pinnick, Glenn Kaiser, Dave and Sue Perkins, Rick and Diana Cua, Phil Madeira, Bob Hartman, Greg Volz, Phil and

Bernadette Keaggy, Kerry and Vicci Livgren, Dave and Kathy Bunker, Randy and Barb Matthews, Becky Volz, Michael Johnston, Mike and Tara Rayburn, Marc Wozniak, Glenda McNally, Norman Miller, Steve and Debbie Taylor, Patsy Moore, Carla Sullivan, Mark Gersmehl, Rick Florian, Billy Smiley, Robin Crow, Geoff Moore, Bill Evans, Neal Morse, Rich Mullins, Mark Heard, Kirk Eberhard, Paul Koopman, Amy Courts, Sixpence None the Richer, Clear, Petra, Small-town Poets, The Waiting, Kansas, The Joe English Band, AD, Ralston Bowles, Chris and Linda Hauser, Fred Caserta, Peter Collins, Tammy Rochelle, Ron Moore, Mark Ferjulian, Mike Rodovsky, Rob Cassells, Shauna Strecker, Paul and Kay Logsdon, Sam Phillips, Matt Slocum, Leigh Bingham Nash, Tim and Barbel Landis, Harry Thomas, Resurrection Band, John Herrin, Greg Carnes, David and Suzanne Martin, Will McFarlane, Amy Grant, Dan and Darlene Brock, Gordon Kennedy, Bill Bachman, David Lipcsomb, Gene and Marni Cotton, Ed and Heidi Nalle, Don Nalle, Mike Nachtigal, Tom Beard, Charlie Peacock, Mark Farner, PFR, Scott Huie, John Gates, Glad, Karl and Becky Mednis, Nancy VanArendonk, Peter York, Holly Benyousky, Ray Ware, Greg and Eileen Menza, Michael Murphy, Chris and Jamie Kearny, Stephen and Lauri Leiweke, Joe Blalock, Greg Oliver, Rob Marshall, Jon Robberson, Mike Blanton, Dan Harrell, Chaz Corzine, David Smallbone, Rebecca St. James, Lang and Renee Bliss, Mo Leverett, Caedmon's Call, Michael Card, Steve Camp, Rick Sandidge, Henry Huang, Billy Sprague, John Huie, T-Bone Burnett, Dan Raines, David Huffman, The Choir, DeGarmo and Key, Bill Hearn, Pat Scholes, Rob and Carol Frazier, Peter and Annie Emerson, James Ward, King's X, Greg and Rebecca Sparks, Barry Graul, Darrell and Janet Harris, Rick and Laura Johnson, Nicholas Tremulis, Kevin Lawson, Tammy Trent, Mike and Patti Mead, Mike Clark, Richard Young, Jeff Roberts, Tom Willett, Charles Doris, and J.D. Wilson.

Warm gratitude to "bidness" partners and employees along

the way: Carey Dodson, Curtis Swartzentruber, Rann Russell, Kurt Andress, Lee Swartz, Chuck and Daphne Schwartz, John Clore, Paul Emery, Jon Bergey, Valorie Buck, Karyl Demonte, Joe Estep, Jeff Gott, Jeremy Gover, Carrie Graham, Morgan Harris, Kelsey Howard Jones, Danielle Kerr, Michelle Kreutner, Adam Kriese, Joy McCaskey, Amber Pettus, Jason Scherer, Michelle Suddeth, Nathan Thompson, Coni Wietmarschen, Hollie Woodruff, Danielle Kerr, Jake Reese, Kristi Rigdon, Howard Bell, Bryan Phillips, Liz Trementozzi, Janie Chu, Denise Kowalewski, Eleanor Caine, Matt Ockerman, Crystal Sinden, Stefani Metranga, Carolyn Lewers, Lisa Michaels, Kristen Lindemann, Rory Daigle, Gail Goforth, Kalli Rasbury, Hannah Spencer, Kyndall Ruby, and Michelle Romeo.

Profound thanks to so many fellow sojourners on the dimly lit path, including: Dan Petraitis, Bob and Jackie Tolford, Michelle Kosik Glawe, Michael Glawe, Vince Wilcox, Melodie and Steve Mull, Jim and Kim Thomas, Devlin and Carol Donaldson, Ben and Elaine Pearson, Dina Capitani, Jim and Melonie Weber, Bill Barnes, Susan Brown, David Dark, Harrison and Deb Taylor, Jay Swartzendruber, James Riley, Amy Dixon, Tony and Peggy Campolo, Kathryn Darden, Jon Trott, Brennan Manning, Donald Miller, Dan Merchant, Sumi Flanagan, Brain Quincy Newcomb, Todd Lake, Benita Walker, Wendy Hannan, Kathy Ervin, Geoff Little, Gwen Moore, Gayle Wakefield, Kathryn and Chris Farrell, Judy Coyle Davis, Duffy and Maggie Robbins, Jeff Spencer, Kevin and Becky Tucker, Allen Clark, Scott and Sherri Leathers, Debbie Coy, Greg Seneff, Lori Lenz, Bart and Marty Campolo, Gay Quisenberry, Andy Neff, David Perry, Catherine Wirth, Sam Russell, Tom and Brenda Holle, Leese Lockmiller, Robin Jones, Lori Loving, Jeff and Carmen Mosely, Katherine Lemos, Laurie Soileau, Sandra Winkleblech, Ron Lambert, Barry Gager, Teri Lewis, Jade Dupre, Karl and Becky Mednis, Reed and Diane Arvin, Melanie Knupp, Dale Burton, Todd Temple, Alison McCommons,

Scott Roley, Jim Long, Dana Russell, Denice Sauber, Linda Schmitz, Frank and Debbie Edmondson, Pete and Claudia Weber, Steve and Annie Wamberg, Erin Sullivant, Sherry Stokes, Kim Maxfield Camp, Carl and Carol Schneider, Kristin Swartzentruber, Suzanna Spring, Kristina Krug, Bill Barnes, Tom and Kim Shumate, Tic Long, Moses Dillard, Grant Beckham, Cindy and Curt Boyer, Mike Furchess, Bruce Brown, Andy Calmes, Mark and Suzanne Townsend, Scott Hatcher, Dick Wulf, Matt and Kirsten Pierson, Wendy Lee Nentwig, Jeff and Molly Jones, Dan and Kari Needham, Joseph Houk, David Alfrey, Bill Decker, Cellblock 303, and my Village Chapel community.

I'm indebted to my Compassion family (past and present): Wally Erickson, Wess Stafford, Dave Olson, Rich Heeren, JoAnn Stroup, Steve Rabey, Isabela Bertoni, Alyssa Stebbing, Mandie Fuqua, Jocelyn Clarambeau, Krissy Thomas, Lee Geysbeek, Mike Severson, Mike Johnson, Roberto Medrano, Rich Van Pelt, Sixto Gamboa, Keith Bordeaux, Stephanie Waldrop, Baum Chonthicha, Julie Johnson, Henri Guarin, Susan Rupia, Spence Smith, Horace Kaaya, Suzie Johnson, Brian Seay, Tim Glenn, Jamie Narwold, Tom Emmons, Doug West, Carmen Notario, Jodi Fuerstenberger, Lydia Frimpong, Karen Taylor, Demisse Wolde, Regina Hopewell, Soledad Agreda, Doug LeBlanc, Helen Panian, Becca Day, Thimothee Guerrier, Paul Sharrow, Bernard Okeke, LaRue Anderson, Grace Kabahueza, Mark Hanlon, Orfa Cerrato, Stacy Johnston, Renee Ladd, Rebecca Thompson, Haydee Ulrich, and Michelle Savage.

I'm also much obliged to radio folks far and wide: Mark Zimmerman, Mike Bingham, Dave Kirby, John Hall, Bruce Everhart, Joe Paulo, Bob Dutko, Frank Franciosi, Shannyn Caldwell, Robin Sullivan, Bill Scott, John Brock, Todd Isberner, Jim Smith, Stephanie Bakke, Jeff Scott, Dave Brooks, Jeremiah Beck, Barry Copeland, Ric McClarey, Dusty Rhodes, Chris Lemke, John Balyo, Dodd Morris, Tim Cardescia, Dave Baker, John Konrad, Tonya Campos, Jack Eason, Tom Lewis, Erin Swanstrom, Joe Battaglia, John Bell, Fred Mc-Naughton, Lisa Landis, Ashlea Brenneman, John Shirk, Kristi Leigh, Stacey Gagne, Phil Smith, Doug Hannah, Brant Hanson, Steve Sunshine, John Owens, Tim McDermott, John Hull, Chuck Pryor, George Plaster, David Stephens, Bob Thornton, Tom Lewis, Brian Mason, Sheila Richards, Rick Davison, Jon Rivers, Kathleen Bensi, Brad Fisk, Marcia Ware, Matt Austin, Ace McKay, Bob Augsburg, Jeff Brown, Donna Cruz, Jim Marshall, David Paul, Tracey Tiernen, Mike Alley, Erin Branham, Chris Courtland, Steve Lawhon, Dick Ireland, David Koch, Len Howser, Tommy Dylan, Brook Taylor, Wily Daunic, Jim Galipeau, Chris Crain, Mark Tordoff, Margaret Colford, Brian Wright, Ronnie Bruce, Mike and Wanda Agee, Chris Staley, Larry Walters, Frank Wright, Jerry and Lisa Grimes, David Fitts, Rob Moore, Christy Pepper Johnson, Dee Etheridge, John Rogers, Jim Burkhart, Anitra Parmele, Drew Powell, Andy Haines, Theresa Ross, Jim and Eunice Hoge, Pierre Chestang, Paul Porter, Jay Johnson, John Block, Jim Campbell, Johanna Antes, Chris Wallace, Dana Shelton, Bridget Sylvester, Jennifer Epperson, Rick Davison, Jerry Brannon, Kevin Steel, Don Schaffer, Jerry Williams, Mike Moran, Mike Blakemore, Kevin Avery, Mike Stout, Paul Anthony, Dick Whitworth, G.W. VanAlstine, Josh Uecker, Joe Buchanan, Ryan Springer, Michelle Strombeck, John Hayden, Collin Lambert, Mark Elstrand, Steve Hiller, Nancy Crane, Dave Jolly, Ken Brooks, Grayson Long, Jeremy and Jill Tracey, Matt Rust, Ray Hashley, Tom Winn, Floyd Turner, Melissa Montana, Don Buettner, Tim Dawson, Kurt Wallace, Tony Silva, Ed Moore, Brenda Hart, Greg Richards, Jim Carter, Doug Moore, Mike Wilson, Derek Gregory, Paula Kay, Joe Polek, Marc Tieschart, Kenny Robinson, Pencil Boone, Becky Wilson, Blanca Vega, Brennan Wimbish, Chris MacCourtney, Paul Edwards, Jack Haveman, Scott Curtis, Brad Lanser, Troy West, Sandi Brown, Scott Taylor, Johnny Stone, Kevin Cottrell, Adam Voysey, Charlie Devine, George Flores, Dave

Armstrong, Kevin McCullough, Tom Michaels, Joe Hunter, Bob Hammond, Mark Shuttleworth, Tom Atema, Jim Kirkland, Alice Knighten, Tom Greene, Jerry Woods, Dwayne Harrison, Gary Moreland, Linda Sennecker, Erica Parkerson, Wally Decker, Verne Hill, Garry Meeks, Marvin Sparks, Eric Johnson, Mark Kordic, Lynsey Fabian, Art Garza, Kelly St. James, Rob Lewis, Mark Jaycox, Dick Lee, Phil Villareal, Scott Saunders, Bill Montgomery, Dan Baughman, Clair Miller, Bill Nance, Tracey Figley, Chris Grindrod, Dany Kayser, Bill Ramsey, Jon Bowlus, John Yoast, Doug Myer, Chuck Gratner, Meg Geissinger, Lizz Ryals, Jeanette Rader, Leighton Leboeuf, Andy Napier, Paul Martin, Mike Perry, Jason Sharp, David Wells, Marisa Lykens, Jonathan Unthank, Mike Miller, Jory Fisher, Barry Armstrong, David Ruhlman, Tom Moyer, Rich Monteith, Derek Cutlip, Chris Wright, John Riley, J.J. Jasper, Marvin Sanders, Ian Punnett, and Scott Keegan.

Besides those already noted in the text, below is more music that moved me or gave solace during my writing bouts: Bruce Springsteen: *Devils and Dust*; U2: *October, Unforgettable Fire, All That You Can't Leave Behind,* and *No Line On The Horizon*; David Wilcox: *Open Hand* and *How Did You Find Me Here?* Transatlantic: *Bridge Across Forever*; Don Henley: *End of the Innocence*; Midnight Oil: *Blue Sky Mine*; Genesis: *The Lamb Lies Down On Broadway*; Mussorgsky: *Pictures At An Exhibition*; Roy Buchanan: *Livestock*; Black Sabbath: *Sabbath Bloody Sabbath*; Emerson Lake and Palmer: *Trilogy*; Simon and Garfunkle: *Greatest Hits*; Liszt: *Hungarian Rhapsodies*; Supertramp: *Crisis? What Crisis?* and *Crime of the Century*; *Jesus Christ Superstar (brown album)*; Bob Bennett: *Lord of the Past*; Frank Marino and Mahogany Rush: *Real Live*; Peter Gabriel: *So* and *Soundtrack to The Last Temptation of Christ*; Bob Dylan: *Oh Mercy*; Bruce Cockburn: *Waiting For A Miracle*; Daniel Lanois: *Acadie*, and *Soundtrack to Slingblade*; Shawn Phillips: *Transcendance*; The Waiting: *Blue Belly Sky*; Neal Morse: *One*; Spock's Beard: *The Kindness of Strangers*; Phil Keaggy: *The Wind and the Wheat*; King's X: *Faith, Hope, Love*; Pearl Jam: *VS*; Live: *Throwing Copper*; Robin Trower: *Bridge of Sighs*; Beatles: *Abbey Road* and *Rubber Soul*; Arvo Part: *Alina*; Monte Montgomery: *Live at Caravan of Dreams*; Yes: *Close to the Edge*; Ashley Cleveland: *Big Town*; The Choir: *Circle Slide*; The Grays: *The Grays*; Pink Floyd: *Wish You Were Here*; Mark Heard: *Stop the Dominoes*; Dave Perkins: *Pistol City Holiness*; Eagles: *Long Road Out of Eden*; Clannad: *Magical Ring*; Sting: *Bring On The Night*; Mike Ferris: *Shout Live!* ; UK: *Danger Money*; Sara Groves: *Tell Me What You Know*; Porcupine Tree: *Fear of a Blank Planet*; Judd and Maggie: *Subjects*; Foo Fighters: *Echoes, Silence, Patience, and Grace*; Waterdeep: *Sink or Swim*; Ralston Bowles: *Carwreck Conversations*; Randy Newman: *Sail Away*; Sacred Steel Convention: *Train Don't Leave Me*; Rick Altizer: *Pop Symphony Scriptures*; Randy Stonehill: *Return to Paradise;* Derek Webb: *Mockingbird*; Debussey: *Pastorales*; Jars of Clay: *Good Monsters*.

Notes/Bibliography

CHAPTER 5

Muse, "Blackout" from *Absolution*, ©2003 Warner Bros. Inc./ Taste Media Ltd. (ASCAP) Lyrics by Matthew Bellamy. Used with permission.

Supertramp, "Even In The Quietest Moments" from *Even In The Quietest Moments*, ©1977 Almo Music Corp / Delicate Music (ASCAP) Written by Rick Davies and Roger Hodgson. Used with permission.

Peter Gabriel, "Mercy Street," from *So*, ©1986 Cliofine Ltd / Hidden Pun Music (BMI) Written by Peter Gabriel and David Rhodes. Used with permission.

U2, "One Tree Hill" from *The Joshua Tree*, 1987 from *The Joshua Tree*, Lyrics ©1987 Chappell Music/U2 / Universal Music Publishing Int'l (ASCAP) Lyrics by Bono. Used with permission.

Elton John, "Don't Let the Sun Go Down On Me," from *Caribou*, ©1972 Universal Polygram International Publishing, Inc. (ASCAP) Written by Elton John and Bernie Taupin. Used with permission.

CHAPTER 6

The Beatles, "Blackbird" from *The White Album,* Lyrics ©1968 Northern Songs Ltd. / Apple Music Publishing, Inc. (BMI) Written by John Lennon and Paul McCartney. Used with permission.

Kansas, "Mysteries and Mayhem" from *Masque,* ©1975 Don Kirshner Music, Inc. (BMI) Written by Kerry Livgren and Steve Walsh. Used with permission.

Muse, "City of Delusion" from *Black Holes and Revelations,* ©2006 W B Music Corp / Warner Chappell Music (ASCAP) Lyrics by Matthew Bellamy. Used with permission.

Emerson, Lake, and Palmer, "The Curse of Baba Yaga" from *Pictures at an Exhibition,* ©1972 TRO Total Music, Inc. (BMI) Written by Greg Lake and Richard Fraser. Used with permission.

Kansas, "Angels Have Fallen," from *Monolith,* ©1979 Don Kirshner Music/ Blackwood Publishing (BMI). Lyrics by Steve Walsh. Used with permission.

CHAPTER 7

Kansas, "Apercu," from *Kansas,* ©1972 Moss Rose Publications, Inc. and Viva Music, Inc. (BMI). ©1973/1974 Don Kirshner Music, Inc. (BMI). Written by Kerry Livgren and Steve Walsh. Used with permission.

Kansas, "Journey From Mariabronne," from *Kansas,* ©1972 Moss Rose Publications, Inc. and Viva Music, Inc. (BMI). ©1973/1974 Don Kirshner Music, Inc. (BMI). Written by Kerry Livgren and Steve Walsh. Used with permission.

Kansas, "Incommudro," from *Song For America,* ©1975 Don Kirshner Music, Inc. (BMI). Lyrics by Kerry Livgren. Used with permission.

Kansas, "The Pinnacle," from *Masque,* ©1975 Don Kirshner Music, Inc. (BMI) Lyrics by Kerry Livgren. Used with permission.

Kansas, "Child of Innocence," from *Masque*, ©1975 Don Kirshner Music, Inc. (BMI) Lyrics by Kerry Livgren. Used with permission.

CHAPTER 8

Kansas, "Carry On Wayward Son," from *Leftoverture*, ©1976 Don Kirshner Music, Inc. (BMI). Lyrics by Kerry Livgren. Used with permission.

Kansas, "The Wall," from *Leftoverture*, ©1976 Don Kirshner Music, Inc. (BMI). Written by Kerry Livgren and Steve Walsh. Used with permission.

Kansas, "Paradox," from *Point of Know Return*, ©1977 Don Kirshner Music, Inc. (BMI). Written by Kerry Livgren and Steve Walsh. Used with permission.

CHAPTER 9

Jethro Tull, "Skating Away On The Thin Ice Of The New Day" from *War Child*, ©1974 Maison Rouge Music / Chrysalis Music Corp. (ASCAP) Lyrics by Ian Anderson. Used with permission.

Kansas, "Hopelessly Human" from *Point of Know Return*, ©1977 Don Kirshner Music, Inc. (BMI). Lyrics by Kerry Livgren. Used with permission.

Kansas, "On the Other Side" from *Monolith,* ©1979 Don Kirshner Music/ Blackwood Publishing (BMI). Lyrics by Kerry Livgren. Used with permission.

Kansas, "Glimpse of Home," from *Monolith,* ©1979 Don Kirshner Music/ Blackwood Publishing (BMI). Lyrics by Kerry Livgren. Used with permission.

Kansas, "Dust In The Wind" from *Point of Know Return*, ©1977 Don Kirshner Music, Inc. (BMI). Lyrics by Kerry Livgren. Used with permission.

CHAPTER 10

Kansas, "Windows" from *Vinyl Confessions*, ©1982 Don Kirshner Music/ Legacy/ Epic, (BMI) Lyrics by Kerry Livgren. Used with permission.

Rush, "Second Nature" from *Hold Your Fire*, ©1987 CORE Music Publishing (CAPAC) / Anthem Group. Lyrics by Neal Peart. Used with permission.

Mark Heard, "Tip Of My Tongue" from *Satellite Sky*, ©1992 Fingerprint Records/ Ideola Music. (ASCAP) Lyrics by Mark Heard. Used with permission.

Police, "Invisible Sun" from *Ghost In The Machine*, ©1981 Chappell Music Company (ASCAP) Lyrics by Sting. Used with permission.

U2, "I Still Haven't Found What I'm Looking For" from *The Joshua Tree*, Lyrics ©1987 Chappell Music/U2. (ASCAP) Lyrics by Bono. Used with permission.

CHAPTER 11

Rick Elias, "Stripped" from *Rick Elias And The Confessions*, ©1990 Carlotta Publishing/ Shiggaion Music. Lyrics by Rick Elias. Used with permission.

U2, "Walk On" from *All That You Can't Leave Behind*, ©2000 Universal International Music BV/ Interscope Records. (ASCAP) Lyrics by Bono. Used with permission.

Jethro Tull, "Wind Up" from *Aqualung,* ©1973 Chrysalis Music (ASCAP) Lyrics by Ian Anderson. Used with permission.

Led Zeppelin, "The Rain Song" from *Houses of the Holy*, ©1973 Syperhype Music. (ASCAP) Written by Jimmy Page and Robert Plant. Used with permission.

CHAPTER 20

David Sancious, "Ever the Same," from *True Stories*, ©1978 Seraphim Music (ASCAP) Lyrics by David Sancious. Used with permission.

Tony Campolo, *Seminar on Science and Culture*, National Youth Workers Convention, Philadelphia, 1987 . Used with permission.

Philip Yancey, *Disappointment With God*, ©1988 Zondervan Books. Used with permission.

C.S. Lewis, *Christian Reflections*, ©1994 Eerdmans Publishing Company. Used with permission.

Kurt Vonnegut, Jr., *Slaughterhouse Five*, ©1969 Dell Publishing, division of Random House, Inc. Used with permission.

Jim Croce, "Time in a Bottle," *Greatest Hits*, ©1973, 1974 Blendingwell Music Inc./ American Broadcasting Music, Inc. (ASCAP) Lyrics by Jim Croce. Used with permission.

Yes, "Sound Chaser," from *Relayer*, ©1974 Topographic Music. (ASCAP) Written by Yes. Used with permission.

Monte Montgomery, "Let's Go," from *Monte Montgomery*, ©2008 Full Moon Face Publishing (BMI) Written by Monte Montgomery. Used with permission.

Yes, "Awaken," from *Going For The One*, Lyrics ©1977 Topographic Music. (ASCAP) Written by Anderson and Howe. Used with permission.

CHAPTER 21

Kansas, "Incommudro," from *Song For America*, ©1975 Don Kirshner Music, Inc. (BMI). Lyrics by Kerry Livgren. Used with permission.

Neil Young, "Old Man" from *Harvest*, ©1978 Silver Fiddle (BMI). Words/Music by Neil Young and Jeff Blackburn. Used with permission.

Genesis, "Ripples" from *A Trick of the Tail*, ©1976 Hidden Pun Music, Inc. (BMI) Written by Rutherford and Banks. Used with permission.

Rush, "Losing It" from *Signals*, ©1982 Core Music Publishing (SESAC) Lyrics by Neal Peart. Used with permission.

Pink Floyd, "Comfortably Numb" from *The Wall*, ©1979 Pink Floyd Music Publishers, Ltd. (BMI), Written by Pink Floyd. Used with permission.

Neil Young, "Out of the Blue" from *Rust Never Sleeps*, ©1979 Silver Fiddle (BMI) Written by Neil Young and Jeff Blackburn. Used with permission.

CHAPTER 24
Kansas, "Lonely Wind" from *Kansas*, ©1972 Moss Rose Publications, Inc. and Viva Music, Inc. (BMI). ©1973/1974 Don Kirshner Music, Inc. (BMI). Lyrics by Steve Walsh. Used with permission.

CHAPTER 26
"Ya Got Trouble" from *The Music Man*, ©1959 Frank Music Corp / Meredith Willson Music (ASCAP) Lyrics by Meredith Willson. Used with permission.

CHAPTER 30
John Hiatt, "Through Your Hands" from *Stolen Moments,* ©1990 Whistling Moon Traveler Music/ Careers Music, Inc. (BMI). Used with permission.

"Blessed Assurance," Fanny Crosby, 1873. Public Domain.

"Swing Low Sweet Chariot" by Wallis Willis, 1850. Public Domain.

CHAPTER 31

Philip Yancey, *Disappointment With God*, ©1988 Zondervan Books. Used with permission.

Parker J. Palmer, *Let Your Life Speak,* ©2000 Jossey–Bass Publishing/ John Wiley & Sons. Used with permission.

LaVergne, TN USA
27 September 2010

198551LV00003B/6/P